SOLO CHOLO UNIVERSITY

A Transformational Handbook

ENRIQUE S. FLORES

Floricanto Press

Floricanto is a trademark of *Floricanto Press*.

Berkeley Press is an imprint of Inter-American Development, Inc.

Floricanto Press

7177 Walnut Canyon Rd.

Moorpark, California 93021

(415) 793-2662

www.*FloricantoPress*.com

ISBN: 978-0-915745-41-8

Library of Congress Control Number: 2020940225

"Por nuestra cultura hablarán nuestros libros.

Our books shall speak for our culture."

Roberto Cabello-Argandoña and Leyla Namazie, Editors

SOLO CHOLO UNIVERSITY

Preface

At age eighteen, I rushed to write this book because I truly believed I would die young, and I wanted to complete this book before my time ran out. I wrote this book in a manner that illustrates and shows how I evolved as a person through different stages in my life. The title was inspired by a friend of mine named Reymundo who took some students on tour to Santa Clara University, and as I approached to meet them in front of the Santa Clara Mission Church, he joked out loud to his group pointing at me, "*And to the right is the University's Resident Cholo, LOL.*"

I was the first barrio *vato, Cholo,* to attend Santa Clara University. I saved my writings of surviving the gang life, surviving a college prep private high school, and surviving in a white upper-middle class campus culture. I kept writings of my troubled gang life, the experience of getting to the university, and surviving the academic rigor and middle-class campus life. I recently found these notes, written over two decades ago, when I was eighteen years old.

I found these notes that I wrote decades ago when I was eighteen years old. They are records of my young life in the inner city, the barrio, and as a gang member. They also foretold the changes I experienced to the point that I broke with the gang, left the barrio, and I found my way to the university. This journey is told from the beginning and each chapter describes the stages I lived and the transformation I went through attending a four-year university in pursuit of a quality education.

CHAPTER 1: Realizing who I was, based on where I came from.

CHAPTER 2: Admitting the need for change, and envisioning a goal in mind, and realizing that getting an education was the means to get there.

CHAPTER 3: Reflecting on my progress, keeping track of how I've changed and improved for the better.

CHAPTER 4: Analyzing myself more in-depth, understanding my beliefs and discovering the root of where my beliefs came from, using a sociological framework.

CHAPTER 5: Getting in touch with my human emotion, in an attempt to break my stubborn, cold heart of stone, to begin the healing process.

CHAPTER 6: Establishing a firm spiritual foundation to strengthen my soul.

I watched the movie "Jesus of Nazareth" over a dozen times, and I reflected on it over and over again until I extracted all of the wisdom and spiritual medicine from the messages.

CHAPTER 7: Healthy questioning about my individual/ personal faith, and constant meditating about the meaning of my existence, because a healthy frame of mind, produces healthy choices and a lifestyle that is life giving.

"THE WISE ONE" True-to-Life sayings and quotes of wisdom collected along the years, (primary sources: Volition. com and The Book of Positive Quotes by John Cook)

Watching the movie: "American History X" and "South Central" really helped me understand the difference between a *homie* and a friend, and about choosing the right mentor, because I firmly believe, "Show me your mentors and I'll show you your future." — Enrique Flores

CHAPTER 8: The commencement of a lifetime of learning and re-discovery.

"I am The Way, The Truth, and The Light of Life"

I chose this title because I think it sums up what I'm trying to do with this book. For instance, I believe this book is "The Way" for many youth deeply involved in gang life to reach their own goal of a better future, their family, and the human Raza in general. Second, I believe I am sharing "The Truth" about what people are thinking, doing, and experiencing behind the "mask." Thirdly, I guess I am "lighting" up the path for all those who choose to pick up my Book, for sharing with the reader what I have learned in my search and journey towards finding "a life worth living."

Why should you read my book?

Well, you will figure that out of yourself as you read along.

My purpose for writing this book is to provide people with my humble advice and to share my story simply. The result I hope to see is to motivate those who live in the hood get educated in Colleges and Universities, a "LatinX Mass Education Movement."

I want Brown Raza to go to the university and achieve positions of influence and power, and then open the doors for other Latinos, and create a better *vida* for our struggling *gente*.

I remember the exact moment in time, a long time ago, when I was about fifteen years old and actually in the ninth grade, talking to my older brother. I told him that I was going to do what my parents wanted me to do and follow the route of going to school. I wanted to see if it's true "what they say" — you know what I mean—those people that say:

"You should go to college" and "Education is the key" and "You should take your time with a girl and be friends first." Blah blah blah...but to my surprise, my brother, said "Okay." From that point on, from that conversation on, my life changed course forever. I went that different route— different from all my homeboys, different from my parents, different from my brother. You see, nobody I knew had ever been to college, had ever attended college, had ever

4

even been to a college campus, much less made it through to college graduation. That idea was too distant, utterly foreign and unrealistic. I had always said to myself, "Fuck, NO! I'm not going to college; I don't got no money." I chose to go this road, not knowing what to expect or how I was going to get there, but I'm here to tell you that my counselor who died (Rest in Paradise) was right.

Rob-dog said to me, "If you go on the right path, doors will open up to you, and behind some of those little doors open up to big rooms!" So here I stand to say to you, "Wake up! And snap out of the same'ol shit. The knowledge I have learned while at Santa Clara University (SCU) was not only for my sake, but I discovered it for you. And throughout this book, I'm bringing the core of the sociological knowledge back to our *gente* who still feel stuck within the barrio walls, to use it as a foundation for all your dreams. To build upon them, so that you can become successful, and make your parents proud— but more importantly— become proud of yourself. I've broken the chains of my self-doubt and stereotypes, believing that "One of us can make it," because one of us did it, so that means two of us can, and if two of us can do it, then that means five people can, etc. There's no limit. I did it, and you, *tú también puedes*. My job is to *"Comfort the disturbed,* [and to] *disturb the comfortable."* —Finley Peter Dunne

Writing exercise 1: What do you think about this book so far? Your first impressions.

Te Doy Gracias

Well, I can't put everybody who has helped me throughout the years in some way, shape, or form. I am going to list those who have positively influenced me, on a deeper personal level, in my efforts to improve myself as a person. I would like to thank and recognize my appreciation and gratitude towards them.

I sincerely thank:

Mi Dios y Nuestra Lady de Guadalupe for never leaving me in my loneliest times and for keeping me safe, long enough for me to finish writing my book. If I were to die, I would like my family to know that I went with a sense of peace/happiness in my heart, and faith in God in my soul, I know I will be called up to heaven once my mission has been accomplished.

My parents and brother: for "letting me go" when I went away to college and did what César Chávez encouraged us to do, "Sal Si Puedes."

All the Jesuit Priests S.J.: Who help me get into both Bellarmine at Santa Clara University, for without them none of this would be possible.

My counselor: Mr. Rob Suarez (R.I.P.): Who help me keep focused during my high school years; and helped put my priorities in the "right" order.

Thank you

Thank you, Tata Dios

For allowing me to wake up this day with my sight, my hearing, my voz;

Thanks for allowing my family members to wake up in good health, instead of a lot of wealth.

Thanks for not giving me the punishment I deserve,

And thanks for giving me the good things of life that I do not deserve.

Writing exercise 2: After reading "Te Doy Gracias"; Who in the past or present would you like to thank? And how did they positively change your life? Who do you owe an apology to?

Chapter 1

Da Myth

I used the title "Da Myth" to kick off chapter one because, for three years, I "disappeared."

I kept away from everybody. I began spending time in the gym for four hours at a time, working full-time, and spending hours in different libraries doing homework. I did all this to avoid getting locked up. If I would have merely "kicked back" with the homeboys in the hood,"… inevitably we'd either find trouble find trouble or trouble would have found us.

When I did a "disappearing act," at least once per year, I would cut off all contact with people, to the point where I would not be seen for months at a time, and people would only rarely give reports of "Silent Sightings." I never took my class picture in high school, nor my "senior portrait" yearbook picture in high school, so that I remained only a "myth" after I graduated from Bellarmine, just like in the streets, after my eighth grade graduation day.

But, as I reflect on my life, the following are the things that I most remember from my experience called life.

- Five years old: First t childhood of love, the first attempt at a French kiss.
- Seven years old: First real French kiss.

- Second grade: First time, I had a knife pulled out on me.

- Third grade: Saw my older brother (My hero) get jumped on his way to school, now I had to worry about his safety.

- Fourth-grade: First wanna-be "gang" I formed in elementary school. The principal talked to me, because I was pointed out as a ringleader, and was told that gangs were not allowed at that elementary school. This just goes to show that the concept of gangs was in my vocabulary at ten years old.

- Fourth grade = While walking home from school, we saw a large crowd gathered on both sides of the side walk at the cross streets of Poco Way and McCreery Ave. As we got closer, I could hear the sound of a woman wailing louder than I've heard anybody scream and cry before. As we walked by, I saw bright red chunks of meat scattered in the middle of the street. I still didn't grasp what was going on. My eyes then focused to the woman screaming and crying. She was sitting on her heels and was holding a toddler on her lap with an open skull and blood soaking both their shirts. I remember seeing this mom rocking back forth wailing and wailing and wailing, because her child was now lifeless and limp. Based on the brain chunks scattered on the street, my guess was that the toddler was hit by a car and fled the scene, because back then, there was no Stop sign at the cross street. No police, no fire truck, no ambulance arrived yet as we walked two more blocks home. We never talked about what happened. Just another tragedy to swallow.

- Fifth grade: First time I got punched in the face and was stunned in shock of what had just happened. But I realized that sometimes you don't know you are in a fight, even when you're getting punched in the face.

- Fifth grade: First time I started packing a pocket knife to walk home with, because I didn't have confidence in my fighting ability, and "everybody else" had bigger knives, so I thought I had a match them, or like my friends, carry a (rusted), deadlier knife.

- Sixth grade: I was outside playing, in the front of our apartments, when we smelled the familiar odor of burning wood. For some reason, it seemed like a different house caught fire at least one time per week. And sadly, it became almost entertainment to go look and join the crowd across the street watching a house burn. Also, back in those days, emergency services (police, fire trucks, and/or ambulance) always took a long time to arrive. So, we walked four blocks towards the thick black and brown smoke clouds, with no sound of sirens. As we turned the corner, we saw the bright flames of the fire engulfing the entire corner house. We stood there— entertained, nosey, then bored. Suddenly we hear family members yelling, "*El bebé! El bebé todavía está adentro!*" And a woman tried to run towards the burning house, with black and brown smoke pouring out of every single window, the ceiling, and the front door as well. "*Se está quemando!*" Then the man that was holding the woman back from going inside, flipped his own switch of courage and he sprinted inside the front door. Everybody in the crowd gasped in horror and the family began screaming even louder. It felt like an eternity as everybody stared at the front door, pushing out the thick black smoke. Again, no emergency vehicles yet had arrived, but far far away, we could hear the sound of a faint siren coming this way we hoped. Then, with a loud crash, we saw the man carrying outside a large crib. This crib however, was blacked by either the fire or painted by the black smoke?

• The man also entered with a white shirt and ran out covered from head to toe in dark brown ash. The yelling erupted again, but this time louder than before—as everybody felt every emotion you can feel seeing all this occurring in real time. The woman, rushed to the crib and pulled up an infant who was not crying, limp, and blackened in appearance. The sound of that woman wailing is recorded permanently in the audio of my memory's ears. The sound of the sirens were now two blocks away. The same man who ran in, after catching his breath, hurried to the mother and grabbed the infant from the mom's arms and began doing CPR while holding the child in his arms. The child's arms and legs still limp. The cries and wailing and sirens now at full volume. The fire fighters then rushed over and took over the CPR effort. The feeling of hope lasted only 30 seconds, until the entire crowd realized that the fire fighters' CPR efforts was not working. A deep sadness fell upon crowd like a fog and everybody began walking back home, swallowing another tragedy we did not speak of, debrief, reflect, or process ever again. Until now—through my writing about it to get that memory out! For about 1 week after that fire, the entire neighborhood was re-traumatized each time we walked by or drove by that street, because the charred infant's crib was still sitting on the front lawn, blackened by the fire and smoke, and also I noticed the broken wooden on the sides that I imagine was broken when the man/the father maybe, pushed the crib forcefully past doorways inside the burning house, blinded by the chocking thick smoke.

- Twelve years old/seventh grade: I wore my first pair of "Ben Davis" pants, and my brother taught me everything he knew about gangs; everything he knew about surviving in a gang war zone.

- Seventh grade: I showed up to a gang rumble, but nothing happened.

- Seventh grade: I was nicknamed "Silent."

- Summer between seventh and eighth grade my brother got stabbed, I learned not to trust anyone 100% and be suspicious of "smiling faces."

- Thirteen years old/eighth grade: First time, I got chased for my life.

- Eighth grade graduation day got stabbed. Lesson learned the hard way: expect the unexpected.

- Summer between eight and ninth grade started weightlifting out of anger and hate in my heart as motivation. The rage lasted three years and was strong enough to stab, shoot, and or kill somebody, anybody.

- Ninth grade, my dad sent me to school at Santa Clara high. The school board didn't permit us because of the boundary bullshit, but we lied and got me in any way. I didn't want to transfer to this school, but I also didn't want to go to Independence, where all my enemies were, and I had no backup. That year I bench pressed 155 pounds max.

- Fifteen years old, the first time I had sex for the first time in more ways than one. I mention this to educate adults that teens are exposed to sexual situations even before they even enter high school.

- Ninth grade first time I smoked weed and cut school after a year of continually saying "It's cool, I'll pass," but I finally gave in after enough peer pressure.

- Tenth grade, I got accepted into Bellarmine, because of my dad's hookups and a lot of people pulling strings, meaning that I was given a chance, against the odds, as the chosen "East Side Project" that year.

- Tenth grade, I bench pressed 205 pounds max.

- Tenth grade, I stopped wearing gang colors. I gave my *paño* away and threw out all my red and maroon *Norteño* clothes and never again supported any colors to this day because I noticed it only made me a target for random gang-related attacks.

- Eleventh-grade bench press 255 pounds max.

- Twelve-grade bench pressed 305 pounds max, which was 100 pounds more than my weight.

- Twelve grade I got into my first real fight. I "won," but I almost messed up my entire chance for a good future, because I couldn't swallow my pride, but more than that, I could no longer hold in everything in—all my emotions that I had bottled up and built up during my "silent-years."

All my hurt, all my anger, all my loneliness, and all my self-doubt due to not knowing how to fight. I took it all out on this one person, making this person unfairly pay for others who wronged me.

- Eighteen years old, I got engaged and grew to care for that person, but it only lasted three months, because I learned you couldn't be with someone just because you NEED to be with "someone" to escape loneliness.

- Eighteen years old, I got accepted into Santa Clara University.

- Eighteen years old, God told me to write a book one morning as I was waking up. The idea popped into my head, and both my heart and my brain felt it was a good idea, so I picked up a pen, and I started writing, and writing, and writing this book.

Writing exercise 3: After reading "Da Myth," please make a timeline history of your life, (like the one I did), of what you remember the most, such as the happiest day or the worst moment in your life, etc.

From da East Side

The mere word "from" is significant and loaded. The primary reason is that what neighborhood you are from, what hometown location you are from, becomes part of your identity. We feel pride proclaiming to be an "East Sider" because it takes a lot of complex body language skills and street smarts knowledge to survive on that side of town.

Nonetheless, I chose these memories, because it describes what a poor brown kid had to learn to endure and adapt to while growing up, which I imagine privileged people do not even have to think about.

I remember the good times during my childhood, such as waking up every Saturday morning to watch my cartoons, like He-man, and G. I. Joe, Voltron, the ninja turtles, and of course, the Bugs Bunny and Tweety Show.

I also remember looking forward to watching the famous Mexican TV show called *El Chavo del Ocho* and *El Chapulín Colorado* and playing the Mexican board game La Lotería. In the latter, we used pinto beans as game pieces and character cards such as La Muerte.

I remember my mom bringing a Mexican sweet bread from the Pink Elephant Panadería, which is still my favorite.

I remember going to Lee's Burgers and Newberry's to play Street Fighter or taking the 22 Bus to Eastridge Mall every week to play Double Dragon or Street Fighter in the big arcade room, drinking a tropical smoothie from Orange Julius. During those years, it was against the rules to wear any red, blue, and maroon clothes inside Eastridge mall. Youngsters could not wear these gang colors inside the mall because of all the gang-related fights and race race-related fist-fights that would occur there almost daily.

But, I also remember fearful and sad times like the big earthquake of 1989. And how I was afraid of the gusty winds when I was in fourth grade, and always worried, praying daily for all my family members to get home safely and soon.

I remember getting inside a smelly disgusting dumpster at age eleven, garbage-picking, looking for aluminum cans to crush and recycle on Story Road located in the heart of East San Jose, California. At age eleven, I also remember buying a squeegee and washing car windows at Tropicana and at King Super to save up enough quarters, dimes, and nickels. I would take a bike ride to east Wienerschnitzel in front of the big Mervyn's store to buy a corndog and some chili fries using the coupons I came over the mail for $.99 each.

I remember how cool kids in elementary school would call me "Goodwill" because I had to wear hand-me-down clothes from strangers. Clothes that my mom's friends didn't need anymore and would give to my mom for us to wear. The funny thing is that I wore it proudly with a smile because it was new to me. I also remember having to share three pairs of pants with my brother and having to wear pro-wings shoes from the Payless Shoe Source by the 7-Eleven instead of Nikes like all the other kids.

I remember not having a big stereo system, but instead having a small ghetto-cassette player with blown-out speakers, a broken antenna, and buttons missing, where I had to use a pen tip to turn up and down the volume. I remember never owning a VCR, and dishwasher, no microwave, and any Nintendo and no Atari. I remember playing bloody knuckles, suicide hand-ball, and quarters, or in our case: pennies, nickels, and dimes.

I remember when the ghetto bird was almost a member of the barrio. I remember listening to the ghetto bird police helicopter nearly every single night, lighting up the hood and my backyard and our living room, with its blueish searchlight, looking for another brown dude fitting the description.

I remember the times when nobody (no kids and no adults) played at parks on the East Side because every single park on the east side was taken over by a gang except Prusch Park. I also remember never hearing any kids play outside after dark.

I remember the times before Susan Hammer became Mayor of San Jose. Then, there were no cops and no fear of police as they were absent from the barrio. The times were Poco Way was in existence. The times before Sureños, before Cambodians, the times when Samoans controlled Poco Way. The times when only Norteños ruled San Jose, so they each divided into sides and picked a color to tell them apart. East Siders claimed the color maroon; North Siders claimed the color red; West Siders claimed the color brown; South Siders claimed the color light grey. But then, one day Sureños wearing blue, moved into Poco Way overnight. First, the Samoans fought against them because they both claimed blue. But then, the Samoans stepped aside and let the *Norteños* take turns fighting against the *Sureños*, but also against each other still, claiming their side of town—all-out warzone. Little by little the Samoans moved down the street. From then on, you would see twenty *Sureños*, running down the street, like the Running of the Bulls event in Spain, with two-by-fours, chains, sticks, and baseball bats chasing my brother and his friend Rude-Dog down the street. No cops would respond to any of this because they were out-numbered. These were times when you would call the cops as a little kid because that's what we were taught in school to do, but the cops would take 45 minutes to show up or wouldn't even bother showing up at all. I timed it once. The times when you did not fear the cops, but instead feared getting caught slipping or empty-handed by a carload of *Sureños*.

I remember walking home from Dorsa Elementary in the fifth grade and standing at the light of Bal Harbor and McCreery Ave across the street from the Jack-in-the-Box and looking at all the Poco Way *Sureños*, posted out there behind the liquor stores. So, I had to go around and take the alternate route home through the alley. The alley between King Super and Pay'n Pack Warehouse. The alley was full of gang-related graffiti/ tagging on both sides of the walls, hundreds of cigarette butts along the cracks and edges of the pavement, broken beer bottles, and the smell of piss and shit all around. The alley was just as dangerous, especially if you got caught right in the middle with no way out. That's how scary it was, and that's why I had to walk real fast and then sprint as I got to the end of it because anybody could be waiting around the corner. That's how I learned to look for shadows on the ground as I approached any building corners by age ten.

And that was only my elementary school years. Now on to my middle school days, where I got transferred to Lee Mathson Middle School from Fisher Middle. Every single morning of my eighth grade year at Mathson was dreadful, never knowing what to expect.

Writing exercise 4: After reading "From da East Side", describe, in detail, your favorite place to be, and explain why it is/was your favorite place?

ENGLISH 002

Feb. 9th. 1998

"Welcome to da Evil Side."

(I decided to use this title because it is interesting how young people take pride in bragging about their neighborhood, city, gang, or side of town as the toughest, most dangerous, craziest, most violent, making themselves seem tougher since that's where they are from.

P.S. I no longer use gang slang as a part of my vocabulary. But this is the way I used to think back in the early 1990s.)

I simply want to reminisce over my entire eighth-grade year and pick out a single typical day of mine to use as an example. And compare a particular experience I had associated with the strongest emotions which the mind is capable of feeling, such as pain, danger, and fear of death. -

To set the scene, I attended Lee Mathson Middle School in the heart of one of the most notorious gang areas in East Side San Jose. I was thirteen- years old at the time and was known by my street-gang-nickname: Silent. In those days, my mentality would be described as "being hard." In other words, meaning that I was in a state of moral numbness, fearless, and emotionally dead while out in the streets.

Well, let me begin by telling a true story about a particular day of mine. I started each morning by putting on my creased and saggy Ben Davis pants, and slipping my favorite folding knife into my back right pocket, for easy access. I would watch my back and keep in constant alert at all times as I walked to school through the rival territory. The walking (pedestrian) bridge over the 680 freeway, a.k.a. "the catwalk," was the most dangerous part of my daily treacherous journey.

One morning, I saw a bigger, older rival, about nineteen-years-old of age pulling out of his driveway. So, as a natural reaction, I challenged him to one-on-one combat, throwing up gang-signs with my hand and fingers. I was only 13 years old, but I was a gotta-be gang member with a knife that I not afraid to use or would hesitate to use because back in those days, I wanted to stab somebody. To continue, the guy got back in his colossal pick-up truck and sped around the block with the sadistic intent of running me over. I could hear his engine roar around the block. I sprinted about half a block, towards my school, to out-run the truck, and I jumped over the chain-link fence and got away. That was my morning, which began with my heart pumping and sweat running down my four head.

Next, there was a lunch-time: which, was usually the current climax of any given school day, with violent fights occurring weekly. I could still envision the puddle of blood that was left on the basketball court one day when a homeboy of ours came onto campus to take care of some business and ended up breaking the rival's nose with one punch.

To give a brief background on the situation at Lee Mathson: there were four active gangs on campus. There was one crip gang, one *Sureño* gang, and two *Norteño* groups. For some reason, I was labeled the leader of one of them. However, on one particular day, a girl began spreading false rumors, instigating tension amongst the four different gangs. As a result, a gang riot almost erupted during lunch-time on the grass field.

Furthermore, I noticed that all of the participants, including myself, had some sort of weapon in their possession. Everything from wooden pool cube sticks, to metal lead pipes, to bike chains, two long belts with metal buckles on the end of them, and of course knives. Witnesses said they saw a handgun or two, plus reports of any enemy caring an electrical stun-gun. Let me stop and remind my readers that these were six, seventh, and eighth graders: ages ranging anywhere from twelve to fourteen years old.

Nonetheless, still old enough to take somebody's life. These pre-teen children, like myself at all at the time, do not fear tomorrow. They refused to consider the consequences of their actions. They proceeded to brainwash themselves and one another to believing that they are indestructible and fearless, which they are successful at because of their increased adrenaline level continuously. All four gangs stood outside in separate groups, two groups on the grass field and two on the cement blacktop. The leader of the crip gang walked in my direction, I approached him as well alone since he was alone. He said, "I don't have any problems with you, it's the other

*Norteño*s we have funk with. So we shook hands in an agreed upon peace agreement. The principal must have been tipped off of the agreed upon rumble that was moments from taking place, because the principal came out to the school yard and announced for everybody to go back to their classes—he was ending the lunch break early today.

Here is a list of just a few school day incidents that occurred during my eighth-grade year at Lee Mathson Middle:

• A desk was set on fire while class was still in session, (I saw the blackened desk outside the classroom the next day after returning from being absent);

• I witnessed numerous fist fights during class time: guys against guys, girls against girls, and even the girl boxing a guy;

• All leading to rumors of hidden cameras being installed in the worst problematic classroom that I was in all year;

• Moreover, the graffiti visible anywhere and everywhere (in the text books, desks, etc.) daily.

• Lastly, two stabbings occurred on school on campus that year.

• The worst feeling of the day was during my last period. I couldn't concentrate in class because butterflies in my stomach, dreading what was going to happen after school this time! Before the bell rang, I used to always tighten-up my shoelaces and make sure I had a shanking tool, whether it be my knife, or a pen, or scissors. And we would take turns peeking outside the classroom door to get a view of the sidewalks outside the fence to see any rivals waiting for us, to then know which way to run home that day. Our model for street survival was to always: "Expected or unexpected." Heeding this warning was a difference between life and death.

I actually had to tell my eighth grade teacher that I couldn't carry my math book home anymore, because I was getting chased after school often by car-loads of rivals or wait for my trouble maker older brother and his homeboys, who would sometimes come after school to pick up their little brothers, or just to catch somebody slipping. So, I told my math teacher that I would have toss my math book over the chain-linked fence, in order to jump over it, and I couldn't afford to pay for it if I lost it. So, she gave me an extra copy to keep in class and the other to keep at home.

One day my friend and I were walking home from school over the catwalk when we spotted older rival gang members down the street carrying a large wooden stick. So my friend and I made a quick left turn down a quiet street going the opposite direction of home. So, we waited for about thirty minutes in those quiet back-streets waiting for those six older rivals to leave and go back into Poco Way. After several more minutes, we decided to attempt to get home before the sun went down and it got dark. As tip toed closer to the end of the street. However, the moment their "look out" saw us, the chase was on. They charge and sprinted towards us like vicious wolves on the hunt. We were chased down the entire block, which seem like an eternity. I don't know if anyone can relate to this, but getting chased is the most horrifying experience someone can possibly go through, especially at thirteen-years-old. Basically because hard-core gang members have no mercy upon their victims. To tell you the truth I was absolutely terrified because there is no doubt in my mind that I would have definitely been brutally beaten to death. Those rivals would have stomped my head against the concrete cement floor until their legs got tired; and/or would have kicked all my teeth out; and/or would have broken in my spine with their heavy wooden sticks; and/or would have each pulled out their stainless steel knives to puncture my lungs; and/or stab me in the neck and leave me to bleed to death.

All of these images flashed through my head as I was running for my life. But as I soon as my friend and I got away by jumping over backyard fences and made it out of that losing situation, we actually went back for retaliation with more heads and back up. So, within five minutes, the experience went from fear into anger and adrenaline excitement. A typical normal day of mine consisted of an overwhelming sense of panic and adrenaline rush until I was safe in bed. So now, it is no surprise that I still have violent nightmares every other night which caused me to swing and kick violently during my sleep. I am not exaggerating in the least bit; I have seen enough savage fights myself and I have heard in the first-hand accounts of war stories to last me a lifetime. The following list of events are just some of the factual reports passed down through the grapevine:

- One day, 40 rival gang members were waiting over the catwalk bridge and pulled out a gun to the head of a 14-year-old classmate of mine.

- Also, two young rivals ages thirteen and seventeen were intentionally run over with a car twice over, resulting in the thirteen-year-old getting all of his teeth crushed out. Consequently, the rival gang believed that I was responsible for the incident, so they placed me on their hit list. No wonder I always stayed home and was not allowed to go out after dark, feeling like a prisoner in my own home, knowing that over 50 rival gang members knew where I lived I wanted a cripple me for life.

- By the age of fifteen, I had already received ten death threats for various reasons. Having your life threatened is a very scary experience because you will find yourself becoming so paranoid, that you cannot help but be nervous about stepping outside your own doorway, fearing an ambush me and my brother would always look out the window before leaving our apartment or even to throw out the garbage. We also made sure to load up my parents cars with at least seven weapons in each car. Since one time, our entire family drove to King Super to buy groceries and when my brother and I got out of the car to walk to the store, five rivals spotted us, so we made a quick U-turn and got back into the car quickly and told my dad to "go-go-go". As my dad pulled out the car in reverse from the parking spot, the five dudes started charging our family car, so my dad had to put the car in reverse and speed out of the parking lot and drove home, 2 blocks away.

- Another rival was beaten with a baseball bat in the presence of his own mother to witness the gang-related attack.

- Closer to home, 30 rivals inside two cars and 1 van, attempted to run over my brother by chasing him with a car on top of the sidewalk, and then one tripped him and the 30 rivals took turns stopping on his body. This just goes to show you how coldhearted and evil people can get, when victims become victimizers. My brother later recounted that his right hand hurt, because the dudes that jumped him were pulling on the iron chain that my brother had wrapped around his hand and wrist but my brother refused to let go because he did not want to get whipped by a chain on top of getting stomped and punched. My brother spent the next week recalling that traumatic attack and trying to envision alternative outcomes. I remember him telling me, that during the attack, he managed to grab on of the enemies in a choke hold and my brother used his forearm to pull as hard as he could on the enemies neck, which caused the larger group of enemies to attack more aggressively, striking the back of his head and back. But I will never forget what my brother told me as portions of his memories began to flashback. My brother told me, "If they were going to kill me, I was going to take one of them out with me."

- In the apartments where we used to live in before (next to pink Elephant), while I was still a baby, my dad told me that our home had been robbed twice, taking everything we had.

- My parents car is an apartment where we live at now has been the target of broken windows, graffiti on our walls, graffiti on the cars, punctured tires, attempted auto theft and attempted home burglary, with the screwdriver marks still dug into the wood on the front door.

- All of this brings about a reaction of anger and retaliation, as well as fear for my family as well.

- Furthermore, my brother and I have been both stabbed in separate occasions. I, myself, was stabbed with a screwdriver twice on my right shoulder, inches from my neck, on my eighth grade graduation day. The list goes on and on.

Sadly, my parents feared for our lives so much, that they took out life insurance on both of us their teenage sons. My dad still blesses me with the sign of the cross before I leave, and my mom tells me from the window to watch my back in Spanish, and this reminds me to never leave without my knife or pepper spray, always pack. Most people believe that East Siders are the least likely to fear anything in life; but, the truth of the matter is, that we are the ones most afraid of circumstances because we know what real life is about and what is capable of happening at any given second that is why we are the most cautious with constant paranoia.

A typical East Sider experiences violence on a daily basis. Personally, I believe getting chased as one of the scariest experiences. Because, in my opinion, to experience of getting chased, is emotional state of knowing that you are about to die savagely. However, if you manage to escape with your life, you will discover the urge to brag about it. For the adrenaline rush at the time of the incident contains feelings of excitement and fun to them as well. Some people actually enjoy their adrenaline rush so much, that they continue to live one risk after another. Undoubtedly, horrifying experiences do affect one's emotions and stability in a negative manner. As a result, the average East Sider becomes hard, emotionally and mentally numb in order to survive on the streets and maintain sanity. Nevertheless, this hardness of heart, mind and soul allows more room to become full of anger, rage, and hate; and, as a result, set themselves lose on society, which they perceive as a punching bag object to take out their aggression. Thus, continuing the cycle of year in popularity of violence.

Writing exercise 5: What is the worst experience you have been through? Have you ever experienced violence or witnessed a violent incident? Or has a family member or close friend ever been the victim of violence? What is your scar story?

Chapter 2

My Dreams

We've always lived in a small apartments. I say that not to complain, because our apartments were always big enough to feel like home, but small enough to know that there was only one bedroom for a family of four. Sometimes we took turns on who got to sleep on the bed. Only two people could fit comfortably and sleep on the bed. It didn't matter who slept on the bed. The first two who got tired and crashed, would sleep on the bed that night. The other two, could either sleep on the floor or choose the couch. But, starting around thirteen years old, I began kicking and punching in my sleep. I found this out, because one night, I woke up kicking my mom. And I decided to sleep on the floor the rest of the night.

I thought it was only a one time incident. But then, another night, I woke up punching my dad in the head. He woke up pissed off, ready to box, but I had to tell him: "Sorry, sorry! sorry! I was dreaming!" in Spanish. My parents always told me they would hear me talk in my sleep and grind my teeth at night too due to all my bottled up tension. From that night forward, I decided to sleep by myself on the floor. When I was about nineteen years old, a girl also told me I swing in my sleep. The sad truth is that between the ages of fourteen to twenty years old, I had a violent nightmares, literally every other night.

Another big fear of mine are ghosts. I've never seen a ghost in real life, and I hope I never do. But I've heard a strange noise at night that was spooky. I always said to myself: if I ever see a ghost, I'll become a monk or altar boy. Meaning that I would want to be as close to God as possible for safety. But then I thought why should it take something like that to get closer to God? In my apartment, we have a small room downstairs small room, but it was too spooky to sleep down there. It was dark, always cold, and away from everyone else upstairs. When I was younger, I would have nightmares of a monster chasing me up the stairs and grabbing my legs, before I got to the top, pulling me down. In my nightmares where I see ghost, I can't yell or talk. I can barely breathe. Sometimes I can't even open my eyes in my dreams to see. I'd panic.

By age 23, I was still scared of the dark. I couldn't be home alone with the lights off. Even with the lights on, my fear would keep me anticipating seeing a ghost come out from the bedroom or walking up from the stairs. I started having ghost nightmares for two years straight, from 20 to twenty two years old; again - every other night. I don't know if anybody can understand or image of what it means to have a frightful nightmare, full of fear and panic, for eight years nonstop, at least four nights a week? Then I heard a preacher on TV say: the devil attacks you the most, and the parts of your life that is a threat to his future. You see, the devil wants to stop the parts of your life that contains hidden strength, where God is about to use and develop, in order to do great things in his world. So I thought to myself: Where is the devil attacking me the most? And I said to myself: the evil one is attacking my mind at night. My mind must be what God wants to use next, to do great things. So I thought, maybe God is allowing me to face my greatest fears at night, in my dreams, in the safety of my home, until I stop being scared. Because once I overcome those two biggest fears, what can stop me? For example, my fear of getting killed by violence, has prevented me from going far from home. From traveling. From going anywhere with crowds for that matter. Going to parties, even graduation ceremonies, limiting my freedom.

Help Against Ghosts

I'm scared to stay home,
All alone;
Especially when it's quiet, too quiet
Silent;
I'm afraid to sleep by myself in the room,
because it always feels like a tomb.
Especially at night with no light,
When darkness frights;
My biggest fear,
Is to see a ghost near,
I'm afraid even to hear;
But I try to think about you-Jesus,
So I can stop being a wuss;
Since my fear is bigger than my faith at night ,
But a couple of times I wanted to fight;
My anger growing stronger than my fear,
And allowed my faith to feel you standing here;
For one night I said with authority and anger in my voice,
"Show yourself it's your choice!"

I <u>AM</u> a child of God!,

And YOU CAN'T touch me! (Got nods);

You can't do me any harm,

Because God calls the shots with his strong firearms;

He's in control,

And he owns my soul.

Writing exercise 6: What do you dream about most? If you don't dream, how old were you when you stopped dreaming? Do you have nightmares? If yes, what about? What do you think your dreams mean? Are your dreams trying to tell you something? Is there a theme?

COMPOSITION AND RHETORIC 1

Dec. 4th, 1997

An essay on the life of an essay

As far back as I can remember, my entire childhood experience has always revolved around gang activity, especially in my East Side San Jose neighborhood, a.k.a. "The Poco Way neighborhood" as the media called it. Those blocks were famously known to be one of the most notorious areas in the city back in the 1980's to early 90's.

My first recollection of violence, during my childhood, is of another second grade boy pulling a knife out on me in elementary school. This first incident was not at all gang related, but it did cause me to become very distrusting and defensive, even to this day. Moreover, I also began caring a small pocket knife for protection while we were walking to and from school. It was at this point in my life, as a matter of fact that I am part of the reputation of being very quiet, serious, mysterious little boy who liked to draw. I was a loner basically because I isolated myself apart from all the other kids due to my low self-esteem.

Yet, I was not officially considered a gang member until the beginning of my seventh grade. Previous to that school year, my brother had always referred to me as "A gangster in a disguise" because I looked like a regular *paisa* kid, but in reality, I was "the look out." But at the age of twelve, my brother took me under his wing and taught me everything he knew about how to survive in a gang warzone. For instance, he made me memorize all the type of cars our rival enemies drove and also where to run if chased, and how to identify rival gang members from three blocks away without any obvious identifiers such as gang colors.

Reminiscing, I recall attending my first real major gang related event, again during my seventh grade school year. My brother and I attended a scheduled rumble that was supposed to take place at a nearby park just before sunset. When my brother and I got to the park I counted over forty heads (thirty two males, three females including three small children brought along to cheer on daddy that would be my guess.) Everyone had some sort of weapon on them: everything from lead pipes, knives, baseball bats, chains, pool-cube sticks, and one single gun, which the leader was packing. I also observed the shot-caller patrolling around the area in his car for any signs of an early ambush or for any police activity. Fortunately, the rival gang we were at anticipating did not show up. Rather, we found out later that they were actually waiting for us at another park, on their turf. This example is just one of the "almost stories" that my entire childhood is composed of.

To this very day, I am still not known by my first name on the street. Rather, I am known by my nickname "Silent" which of course comes with the reputation of being a gang member, a very sexually promiscuous player, a wallet thief, mute, and a prejudiced racist.

Writing exercise 7: What's your reputation? What would your teachers say about you? What would your parents say about you? What would your friends say about you? What would others say that you care about most? Are you okay with these descriptions of you? What part of your reputation would you like to change?

Poco Way, please go Away

To good to be true,
Can't believe Poco Way is through;
All that never-ending fear,
the police and their helicopters protection never near.
hearing the gunshots,
and the yelling of those chasing and getting chased across the parking lot.

telling my mom to duck and turn off the lights,
and to get away from the windows day and night.

people still do not fully understand the seriousness in my voice when I say:
I learned this in order to survive;

because at that time, I thought for sure, my brother was going to die.
why do you think my parents got life insurance for both her teenage sons, praying never having to say goodbye?

my dad still blesses me with the sign of the cross, and mom tells me from the window in Spanish: "Watch your back",
and it reminds me to never leave without my knife and pepper spray, always pack.

hence, my life seems like a dream, never completely free,
because deep down inside, I still expect things will return back to normal you'll see.

It is like a big earthquake that hit once before and pressure building every summer that is quiet,
or like a thief that has broken in and is gone, but believing he will come back, when you least expect it.

reminiscing about constantly worrying about my brother
out there gang banging at Overfelt and in the street, never under cover;

reminiscing about getting paged 911-13-22,
which translates into homeboy emergency/need a back-up fast/rivals involved/bring the .22 semi-up auto too.

instead of a bracelet, I used to give my girlfriends pepper spray,
and my brother knives to pack every day.

but nevertheless I have to admit I would never call any other place home,
even though I lived in SCU for four years, and have

been going to school in Santa Clara for the past eight
years, alone.

I hear about the size of LA,
and I'm afraid that it's worse than Poco Way.

I was twelve years old, they were fifty deep, no cops, no
po-po's;
now, I am twenty one, stronger physically, yet weak
mentally. I don't know how to fight, but I know
I need to know;

ever since I bought a gun
I don't feel helpless anymore, nor run;

when you start believing it is safe, to relax, smile, to
enjoy life, and let your guard down, just hang,
it is then, that you are slipping, not ready, not on your
toes, not angry enough to react in one second, bang!

Writing exercise 8: What do you wish would simply disappear, just go away? How would your life be better? How can you avoid that person, place, or thing that is harmful?

Silent vs. Enrique

So, who am I? Who was I? And who do I want to become? Well I start off by telling you who I used to be. When I was in seventh grade I was nicknamed "Silent" because I did not smile, I did not laugh, I did not talk more than a couple words at a time, and when I did a talk people around me would turn around and with a surprised tone in their voice would say out loud, "Damn he does talk!" I was silent until my senior year in high school. As Silent I could not look at anybody in their eyes. If someone were to look at me I would turn away or look at the floor. I get irritated because they were staring at me for too long and I wouldn't tell them "What?!." I realized I didn't want my good teachers to see the hate in my eyes.

I wasn't happy and had not been for a very long time. I started studying myself to see why I was the way I was and I figured out it was because of my childhood years when I was always picked last for kickball or not picked at all. I was made fun of and ridiculed because I would get picked up from school in an old ugly bright orange Ford Pinto that my family owned. The kids would call it "a cardboard box with wheels." The sad fact is that negative comments can be so traumatic that even one ugly word can last a lifetime. It's been said that the past is the past and unless you continue to remember it and bring the hurt back with you into the present. Consequently, this was a root of my own low self-esteem. I tortured myself for seven years of my life by recalling the words that I heard throughout my childhood. Words that were used to describe me, such as, being told I was "Stupid", "Slow", "Boring", "Annoying", and "Ugly." But what was even worse than being called all those hurtful words, was me believing them, and seeing those words in the mirror.

I think it all started when my family was too poor to afford the name-brand clothes and too poor to even afford hair clippers. Or even a stylish haircut at the barber shop. So I had to use hand scissors to cut my own hair which I always manage to leave uneven bald spots. Thus with no shred of self-confidence, a horrible self-image, and zero self-esteem, I gave up all the hope. Hence falling into a deep state of self-pity and remained for seven years of my life. Where in that time span I became almost mute, even to my own family, convinced I had nothing good to say. Which resulted in me vanishing from society in general and retreated into my own little world.

But then I started going through a bunch of mood swings, emotionally unstable and confused of why I was so angry. People actually told me that I had multiple personalities because I would be all cheerful and nice one minute and then all of a sudden angry and defensive the next second, then suddenly sexually flirtatious, and lastly sad and depressed the next. I wouldn't jump back-and-forth from six different personalities/moods. I finally figured out where three moods each for two different separate categories Silent versus Enrique.

To compare them both:

Silent:

1.) Number one on the list is a sex addict that will have sex with any adult female. It didn't matter if I thought they were too old or too ugly, it didn't matter, I just needed a release. I started realizing I had no standards, no control even though I knew it wasn't smart to have unprotected sex but I also couldn't afford to continuously keep purchasing packs of condoms. Nevertheless I always received praises and props from my male comrades because of my sexual conquests.

2.) Always angry, pissed off, ready to fight with the any human being no matter how big. Listening to hard-core rap music, like Brother Lynch to get me pumped up and speeding recklessly in my car driving with road rage and daydreaming about a bunch of violence sadistic thoughts and scenarios. Hard-core rap music always affected my mood and always brainwashed me to be more violent. But I believed I needed to stay pissed off because anger kept me alert and ready to fight when faced with a spontaneous threat. I noticed the more I fed my anger emotion the less room there was left in me for compassion and mercy.

3.) Always tense, irritable, stressed out, feeling empty inside, emotionally dead, with my conscience turned off to the point where I witnessed my homeboy kicking his dog because he said his pitbull was a little bitch and not tough enough. A slapping the dogs head with the bell and stepping on the dog's neck and seeing that animal cruelty it didn't faze me. I didn't feel any compassion when I believe I should have felt something—anything, especially when a helpless animal suffering and in pain.

Enrique:

(I discovered when my heart began coming back to life around the age of eighteen.)

1.) Depressed. Super sensitive to getting my feelings hurt. Would cry a lot when rejected, seeking love, intimacy, and physical affection. Always listening to oldies.

2.) Slow mentally. Naïve, like a little kid, goofy, friendly, very gullible/trusting, a perfect gentleman. Enjoy listening to Mexican music.

3.) Very religious. Spending quality time with my family, listening to church music, praying, super aware of death, so always paranoid! Most of these things characteristics I mentioned above under "Enrique" are emotions and behaviors that considered "Weak Sauce" in the streets - that is why most people do not admit to them and/or have condition themselves not to feel these things. It took me a long time to finally discover what's inside myself (the good, the bad, and the shameful) to see where I am now and see how much further I have to go to fix myself up and improve myself into the person I wanted to become. But sometimes a flesh is weak. You want to do good but your lustful body takes over because you still don't have the self-control yet your willpower isn't strong enough yet. But I knew I couldn't give up, because I learned that even the Saints back in the day struggle to become good. For example the apostle Paul said, *"I am a slave to sin. I do not understand what I do. For what I want to do I do not do, but what I hate I do. And if I do what I do not want to do, I agree that it is no longer I myself who do it, but it is the sin living in me. For I have the desire to do what is good but I cannot carry it out, for what I do is not the good I want to do; no, the evil I do not want to do - this I keep on doing. What a wretched man I am! Who will rescue me from this body of death?"* (Romans 7:14-24.)

Well that's a question you have to answer for yourself. Personally, I need to trust in something, someone higher than myself; because I can't control what happens. I can't control my health. I can't keep somebody from dying. I can't snap my fingers and make things get better all by myself.

So what kept me on participating in gang violence? Well, the main reasons were the tears I wiped away from my own mother's eyes when I saw and heard her cry when my brother got stabbed is what broke my heart and kept me from putting myself in harm's way. Because I thought to myself, "Who am I going to hurt the most if I get locked up for years? Who is going to hurt the most if I get fatally stabbed in the neck or if I get shot in the lungs where I can't breathe or get permanent brain damage from getting hit in the head with a baseball bat? Well? Tell me who?

I guarantee you, your mom, your sweet *jefita* will be the one to suffer the most and cry and scream and can't eat, can't sleep, and go into depression with nightmares because a piece of her heart has been taken away from her.

It takes a lot of guts and courage to change. It means resisting peer pressure and standing up on your own without relying on a bunch of homies to hold your hand and make you feel like you're all big and mighty. The only opinions that matter and that you should care about are those of the people that don't encourage you to defend your reputation a fight. Those people that don't offer you drugs, beer, or cigarettes. But instead listen to those people that do offer to help you get a job, those people that do ask you if you want to go to church with them, those people that do beg you to squash it and to please don't go do anything in retaliation. The movie that helped me see this difference most clearly was the old school movie: "South Central".

Quotes:

"Even a fool is thought wise if he keeps Silent." —Proverbs 17:28

"Show me your friends and I'll tell you who you are." — Mexican Proverb

"If you don't know who you truly are, you'll never know what you really want." —Roy T. Bennett

Writing exercise 9: After reading "Silent vs. Enrique,"answer the following: How do you act at home? How do you behave at school/work? How do you act around your friends? How about around the opposite gender? Do you act the same in all the settings? Or different? If different, which is the real you? And which ones are just masks? Choose five words that would best describe the true you.

My drawings

I have very few surviving drawings, those I did not throw away. I was always and am, my own worst critic. I always drew out of emotion. A lot of my drawings, I drew while feeling depressed. But, I created a rose drawing that took me like 2 weeks to complete. That rose was actually my first happy drawing, because I used to only draw pictures that reflected my anger, sadness, and the gang lifestyle that I glorified.

I guess I like drawing so much because it was my emotional outlet, my self-administered art therapy I desperately needed to vent my suppressed emotions.

I drew a clock once in art class in tenth grade, but I didn't think much about the time I drew on it. But when somebody asked me why I chose to draw the time as 3:27, I didn't know the answer. And since I don't believe in accidents, I decided to search the Bible for any chapter 3's and verse 27's. But, I only found one, no matter how hard I tried to find other options. And it was in Proverbs. Proverbs 3:27. I'm sure there's another 3:27 somewhere, but I thought the one in Proverbs was perfect. Maybe serving as a foreshadow?

Proverb 3:27

"Do not withhold good from those who deserve it when it is in your power to help them."

Writing exercise 10: After reading "My Drawings", what do you do to vent/express/release your bottled up emotions? How is it helpful? What else can you try to heal?

Chapter 3

Stubborn about changing?

I used to go apply at Togo's, McDonald's, Lucky's to apply for jobs and wonder why they wouldn't call me back like they said they would. One day it dawned on me, maybe it is because I would walk in wearing my cut off (creased) sweats, a white tank top, and a beanie on my head low over my eyes or dark locz sunglasses—walking in with the hard look on my face, asking for a customer service application.

But I was stubborn. I used to tell myself, "I'm not going to be fake? This is the way I am. Why should I try to change and be somebody I'm not. Fuck these people and what they think. I didn't want their stupid job any fucking Waze!"

So I kept my pride, but I stayed unemployed as well. But, little by little, once I chose to get used to certain things, like wearing a tie, get to class on time, or saying excuse me sir, once, twice, three times, enough times over and over again, it started becoming a part of me. But, if you don't believe me, find out for yourself and see how you're treated when you act, dress, and talk one way versus the opposite way.

For example, when I was working at my security job, I wouldn't ask for a break, and the white boss said to me, "You got a break when you got hired here." Then he tried to set me up to sell him weed, and I filed a three-page complaint letter against him to someone higher up, because everyone has a boss. And in the last line of the letter I said I conduct myself in a professional manner and I expect to be treated with the utmost respect. Or something like that, but the point is I won, because the next day that fool was all kissing my ass every day after that. Trust me, there's better ways to taking care of someone, then just socking them up, without getting yourself fired, or locked up, Or having to pay fines are all of the above.

Quotes:

"It ain't what they call you, it's what you answer to." —W.C. Fields

"My life is in the hands of any fool who makes me lose my temper." —Joseph Hunter

Writing exercise 11: What's your dream job? Something you'd never get bored doing?

Employment

The way I see it: first show me the effort, then I'll show you somebody who cares. I used to go over to my homeboy's house and see my homeboy sitting on the couch is talking about "Hey Silent, hook me up with the job!" But, after a while, what I noticed is that everyone wants a job hook up, but nobody wants to work!

I used to hook up homeboys with jobs over and over again, but often the next day they didn't show up to work, talking about, "It was too hot", or "It's too early", or "It's too boring." Excuses are always easy. Because if you want something bad enough, you'd walk all night to make sure you are there on time. Nobody ever says it's too hot to go cruising or go to the summer fairgrounds or too early to go meet up with a girl and get laid. Excuses don't get you pay checks.

I believe once you've experienced real hard work, then, and only then, will you be able to fully appreciate a boring job. I learned the hard way, so now I don't complain about having to sit down all day on the cushy chair, in an air-conditioned office.

For example, here's a list of some of the jobs I've done in my life ever since I started working for the first time at the age of eleven:

- Eleven   years old: washing car windows at Tropicana plus garbage picking inside smelly dumpsters in order to recycle aluminum cans.

- Thirteen years old: cleaning backyards in private homes, when I was going to the unemployment office every morning, located on Alum Rock and King Road, across the street from Church's Chicken.

- Fifteen years old: door to door sales, selling candy and almost getting bit by dogs. I was working on pure commission, that means if I worked all day and if I didn't sell anything, I didn't take home any money.

- Sixteen years old: foreman/painter. I used to get up before 6am each morning after looking at the city map and bus map/route times the night before and then take 2-3 buses and walk to a different address each week. Near or far, sometimes to Saratoga, sometimes to Cupertino, sometimes to Milpitas. So, who's going to tell me that it's impossible because "It's too far and I don't have a ride?" And every time I used to go to a different part of town, I was surprised that none of the houses had iron bars on the windows or doors. Not only that, I was also amazed at how big the houses were and, since I've never lived in an actual house, only apartments. When I got to these rich neighborhoods, I used to say to myself, damn! Six East Side houses would fit where the house is at! Two houses would fit in the huge front yard, two houses would fit inside the actual house, and two more houses would easily fit in the big backyard. But, not only that, I was also amazed at how much wealth people had and how they responded to me. For example, one person called the cops on me when I was just standing out in the public street waiting for my (painter) coworker. When I asked him why he was keeping an eye on me, he said "We usually don't have people like you just standing around here."

• Seventeen years old: painter/foreman. I used to start sweating before I even started, setting up the equipment, officially starting to work at 8am in the morning and not finishing till sundown, sometimes without a lunch break. I was scared of heights, but I still had to climb a wobbly two-story latter is, in the 102° degree hot sun on my face and not being able to hold on to the latter because I had a sprayer one hand, and the shield in the other hand. Relying on my tired legs and balance to keep me alive. One time I almost fell off the roof, hanging over the edge, yelling out for my coworker, but he didn't hear me, so I had to manage to get myself back up with all my strength and staying calm.

• Nineteen years old: sitting on my ass in an air-conditioned office as a security guard at the reception at desk, where I taught myself how to type with two hands one summer, using a blank piece of binder paper and I drew all the letters from the key board onto little squares I drew.

• Twenty years old: the Home Depot doing manual labor, carrying bags and bags of manure, and loading up hundreds of large bricks all day, every day during the busy season.

Once, I got my foot in the door officially hired, I reminded myself of the words I used to tell my homies: "Once employed, always employed." —EF, meaning that if you don't like your job, get a better one, before you quit the first one.

From experience, I also learned that there are only two reasons why most people get fired:

1.) You Do Something Wrong: You don't follow directions, fighting, stealing something, fail the drug test, you did not act in a professional manner, meaning you cuss or are rude or get an attitude, or short tempered.

2.) You Don't Put In Enough Effort: You don't show enthusiasm: you call off sick a lot, you come in late more than a couple times. I'm telling you, if you want to keep her job, you have to go beyond the minimum and be polite at all times, friendly, and smile and be willing to help other people, even if it's not your job to do it. Jobs now focus a lot on teamwork and customer service. When I first started my cheek muscles would physically hurt at the end of the day, because I wasn't used to smiling that damn much!

Quote:

"If you want something you've never had, you must be willing to do something you've never done." — Thomas Jefferson

Writing exercise 12: What do you think you need to/ should: Stop doing, Start doing, Keep doing, do Less, and do More of, to improve your life? To be safer, healthier, and happier.

King and Story

Here is a real life story,
that takes place every single morning, even if it's raining
and pouring.

Of unrecognized heroes,
also known as Day Workers, who the government
considers illegal zeros.

This story starts off each morning at 6 am,
with over 200 immigrant men.

Wondering if *"cobijas de los pobres* will rise from the east,
the street curb serves as a comfy seat.

Muchos duermen a los cuatro vientos, exposed to the four
winds outside,
but the hope of work today will wake them before they
die."
When I go drop off food here and there—*a los tantos,*
the first words out of their mouth is *cuantos*!?

Which translates into: how many workers do you need?
The desperation of their voice, because they have
children to feed;

I do not hear: do you have any spare-change?,
Like those who hold out their soft skin palm - refusing
the change;

Like the American man by the freeway holding the sign
without fear:
"Why lie, I want beer";

Yeah, people gave that fool money - his smile still
growing,
in contrast, the *trabajadores* receive daily police
harassment for the sin of loitering.

Writing exercise 13: What thoughts and feelings came up for you as you read the poem "Story and King"? Which were your favorite lines/statements?

My School Experience

I went to Dorsa for elementary, Fischer and Mathson for middle school, Independence for summer school, Santa Clara High for my freshman year, and I graduated from Bellarmine College Preparatory. I am now currently enrolled at Santa Clara University full-time, going on my third year. I'm taking it slow, a comfortable pace. I've got about a C+ average. The way I see it, if you graduate with an A+, or C, it's still the same piece of paper, que-no? Unless, of course, the path to become a doctor or something, then that's different. But for me, my philosophy is "C's get Degrees."

What I noticed from attending public schools on the east side, is that you learned about everything, but studying. You learn about what gangs are all about, you learned never to talk shit, you learn how to watch your back, you learned what not to go, you learn all about sex and who's down to give it up, you learn how to dress without double creases and with matching colors, and you learn how to tag right. On the east side, white people are the minority. On the east side, I never saw nobody with the book in her hand, much less ever reading during lunch time at school. On the east side, nobody ever talked about college, or "What grade did you get on the test?," or are you going to France for vacation again this summer? Nope, never. It just wasn't cool. Well, that's exactly what I started hearing when I got to Bellarmine.

70

When I walked onto the campus of Bellarmine, it look like a park. But better than the parks I knew, because Bellarmine's campus actually had a green grass! And not a single mark of graffiti or tagging or nothing, the walls were hella clean. There were colorful flowers around all the trees and shit! It was crazy! Then I saw the thousands of white boys that go there, and I was like, what the fuck!

Where all these white boys come from!?. I didn't know that many white people even existed. I was shocked. It's called a cultural shock. Because on the east side, all you see our Mexican people, brown people, brown poor people. In Santa Clara I saw brown people, but they weren't East Side type of people. In my opinion, when I heard them speak and saw that way they acted, I called them coconuts, sellouts, and white-washed. I would get angry at them when I heard them claim to know about gangs or when they claimed to be from the East Side too.

You can tell who knows what's up, because it takes one to know one. I've heard fools say, "I know the East Side, I went to school there, or I go visit homeboys over there, or I go cruising at a party over there," blah blah blah. The way I see it, if you're in a hurry to get there, you are not from there. There's a big difference between going to visit, and actually having no choice but to live there day in and day out. We don't have the option of going home to Santa Clara or some other safe neighborhood and having a nice dinner when things get rough and dangerous.

I'm tired of wannabes coming to the East Side and starting shit with *Sureños*,,(like hitting an active wasp hive for us to deal with because we have to live there) and do not have the option of going home and sleeping in the quiet, middle-class neighborhood and bragging about it the next day or month. We live in the barrio, we live in the hood, we live in the ghetto, we live in a whole other world. A whole other subculture. In the concrete jungle.

But God has a funny sense of humor, because I ended up transferring into Bellarmine for tenth grade of all places. It was like night and day, totally and completely, opposite and different from everything I was used to. The bushes were trimmed perfectly, too perfect. The whole campus was so perfect it all got on my nerves. As soon as I got there, I decided I wasn't going to conform or become weak and lose my edge, my street smarts. I was determined to stay true and represent as a solo-cholo. I refuse to participate in sports, or in class skits. I would always play the tree, meaning that I would only stand on the side.

The thing that pissed me off the most, was when they told me that I had to shave off my mustache, because it was a school rule. I've had a full mustache since I was in 8th grade. To me, I took that as an insult. To me, they were trying to make me look like an all-American boy. So the more they tried, the more I challenge their efforts. I convinced doctors to write letters for me explaining that I couldn't shave it because of a skin irritation. I wrote protest letters to the principal of the school explained that a mustache was an important part of my

Mexican culture, since my father had a mustache, all my uncles had mustaches, most of our Mexican heroes had a mustaches. But, I don't think they even realized the fact that my mustache meant more to me than my fucking grades!

Most times I refuse to shave it off. But when I did, I just told myself it will grow back thicker, I couldn't even look at myself in the mirror. It was like somebody shaving off my eyebrows. I looked different. I was so uncomfortable with my appearance that I would wear a beanie on my head even during the summer, or put on black locz sunglasses to improve my appearance. The sad fact is that I didn't like the way I look even before Bellarmine. I didn't like the way I looked when I smiled. I didn't like the way I sounded when I talked. So, I kept in the shadows.

And sure I hated it at Bellarmine, but I obeyed my father. The only thing that kept me from quitting, was my mom and dad's hopes and dreams on my shoulders. I felt the same when I got to Santa Clara University. I felt like everybody looked at me like I was a vicious, strange looking, zoo animal about to strike. I guarantee you I was not happy each and every morning, for the four years that I had to wake up at 6am sharp, eat cream of wheat which I hated, but my dad kept insisting that it was healthy. And did I mention I only had 25 minutes to wake up from a deep sleep, eat my cream of wheat for breakfast, get dressed and be out the door. In 25 minutes! If not, I knew my dad wasn't bluffing when he would say he would leave without me, and I didn't want to take two buses for 2 hours to get to school. So, it is needless to say that I learn discipline that first year, then self-discipline. I followed my own advice, as I always "Do as you ought to, not as you want to." (Benjamin Franklin).

Selfishly, I wanted to go to public school on the East Side like everybody else. I told myself I was missing out on lots of sex, kicking back with the homeboys, and my overall youth. But, when I think about it now, what did I really miss out on? - besides getting locked up for murder; besides getting kicked out of a dozen different schools; besides killing a few hundred brain cells trying out all of the different new drugs; besides getting a bunch of girls pregnant and catching a couple more STDs. Basically I didn't like Bellarmine but I got used to it.

Out of embarrassment of going to an all boy, white boy, private school, I told my homeboys on the east side that I was attending Santa Clara high school and I told my San Jonero homeboys who lived in Santa Clara, that I attended Overfelt high school. And if they saw me at a bus stop near Bellarmine, I would lie and say that I was coming from the motel, after "visiting" with a girlfriend, which they believed because of my reputation.

In truth, when I first got to Bellarmine, if somebody would have given me a white canvas and told me to paint a picture of whatever I wanted, using any colors I wanted, I would have most likely, painted in dark, black and maroon colors. Because of all the anger I had bottled up and gang mindset I had at that time. But, as time went by, years actually, I started to look at and noticed the other colors that were there, available for me to use. Before, I used to think (or was

74

conditioned to believe) that the color yellow was a sissy-lala color, and blue, fuck blue, were for my rivals. But then, I was in an art class my senior year, and I started using all the colors that existed, especially the bright colors to paint nature scenes.

I like nature. It's relaxing to me. I like green green grass, and painting a bright yellow sunny sun coming up, rising from the mighty East Side. But, I also started to like the way the color blue looked when I painted a blue sky and the blue ocean. It was a nice looking color I thought. It was a color God made to. And I started to ask myself and think why? Why did I hate that color so much? It wasn't the colors fault. Now I color in any and all colors that I want, because true vatos know that wearing colors don't make you down. It's what's on the inside that peoples respect you for.

Bellarmine, provided a place where I could feel safe and not to be scared to act the way I wanted to act, or say what I wanted to say. I finally began to open up my twelve grade year. Attending Bellarmine served as a metamorphosis process for me. I went through a transformation process, like a butterfly from a cocoon emerging after getting enough self-confidence to break free. I noticed that there was nobody to impress here with my big mighty gang banger attitude. Except myself.

The teachers never treated me like a kid, but rather as an adult, who was experienced about life since I never really had a normal adolescence/teen years. Unfortunately, I went from my childhood, to worrying about grown-up stuff like work, sex, safety, and respect. But at Bellarmine, I had a lot of time to think. To step out of my old way of thinking, and to see myself and my life and the east side from the outside looking in, but still as an insider. I saw that what was important on the east side, was not important at Bellarmine. Because watching my back and supporting colors at Bellarmine serve no purpose; but, on the other hand, studying for a test was of the utmost importance.

So, I started dropping parts of my gang member identity, to make room for my new identity: that is a student. Hence in twelveth grade, I finally decided to stop wearing colors. And I made a list of all my sinful stuff I was doing that I wanted to stop doing. And I crossed/check them off, one at a time, such as: cussing, stealing, and my sex addiction, which was the hardest kick and took many relapses. During my lonely walks to school each morning, Jesus became like my imaginary best friend. As I went from talking to myself, to talking to God.

I went from being, first: An East Sider who goes to school, to eventually becoming a school boy, who's from the east side. As a result of my stint there at Bellarmine, and having a lot of time to think. I am proud to say that I am no longer a dirty wallet thief like I used to be, and I am no longer prejudiced and racist towards whites, blacks, or Asians. I made all kinds of friends at Bellarmine from all kinds of races: Portuguese, Filipino, mix, etc. They treated me respectfully and definitely are funny peoples. And, during my twelveth grade senior retreat, called KAIROS - which means and translates into "Time with God", I realized how much I have changed, throughout those three years I attended Bellarmine.

But, I am not going to lie to you, many times I wanted to return to the hood to kick back with the homeboys, because there, and only there, did I ever feel I was 100% accepted the way I was. I would often get fed up with all those jolly, happy, annoying, dorky ass, *joto* acting white people in this upper class Ivy League school. But, that's exactly why we need more diversity to learn from, to learn that "different doesn't equal wrong." Because life, your life, is much more than just the East Side. You have to be able to look beyond Berryessa Road, to look beyond White Road, to look beyond Eastridge Mall, to look beyond King Road, to look beyond the 101 freeway, to look beyond downtown, there are no limit to how far you can go. Trust me, as long as you have the ganas, the enthusiasm, the heart, the passion to succeed, you already have.

Being all alone, that was the biggest problem I faced. So, the goal for you is to take a homeboy or homegirl with you and walk side-by-side together: relating to each other, struggling together, supporting each other, encouraging each other, helping each other. But please don't complain about a lot of homework. I discovered that a lot of homework only prepared me for college, which helped me adjust to the workload easier. So, the teachers are actually doing you a favor; because, if they go easy on you, and you want to go to college and make it through college, the stress is going to be too much of a shock. School isn't easy, but it's not impossible.

It's not that it's hard, it just takes a lot of time. You have to give up almost everything else if you don't know how to manage and organize your time right. School becomes your life for a couple of years. Okay, okay, about eight years! Four in high school, and four in college. But, if I can do it, and did a blindly with no guide, you can surely do it too, now that you got this roadmap to light your path.

Don't be fooled, and I'm not at all that smart. I flunked a couple of classes; I flunked lots of tests; I needed several tutors to hold my hand and answer all my questions, especially in math and science, because I'm kind of slow in the head sometimes. I get frustrated, I get bored studying and take a lot of breaks, or else my eyes begin to hurt. As you can see, a notice, a little nerd, and it has rubbed off on me throughout the years. Since I will be talking with all these big words now. Lol. And, it's a trip the way things have changed for me ever since I started going to college.

I went from begging for someone to give me a job, and getting turned down, like when I got rejected twice from McDonald's and twice from Togo's; but now, that people know I go to Santa Clara University, I'm being offered so many job opportunities, that I'm turning these jobs down. I even turned down three jobs in one week once.

Quote:

- *"I am not retreating. I am advancing in another direction."*—Douglas MacArthur

Writing exercise 14: What motivated the author to get involved with gangs? And are some other reasons why young people get involved and stay involved with gangs?

Chapter 4

COMPOSITION AND RHETORIC 1

(Final: Self-Evaluation)
De. 5th, 1997

Me and My Writing

As I selected the main entry for my final portfolio, I consider the question to answer: Which one of these papers tells more about who I am? I finally decided on the following paper: An essay on the life of an Ese. I chose "An Essay on the life of an Ese" because I wanted people to discover that not everybody lives a wholesome, carefree, nurturing, financially stable lifestyle. Moreover, I also wanted people to know that there is still hope for a kid from the ghetto - provided that people care enough to lend their support to help underprivileged youth succeed, such as myself. While most kids in elementary school we're learning about dinosaurs and how to play Nintendo, I was learning how to watch my back for an attempted attack and learning how to make homemade weapons or sharpening tips a screwdriver or hammering nails into two by four's.

Everything I wrote, I wrote for a reason. I kept my alter-ego Silent because I needed my edge. I needed to remember getting hurt for me to recognize it coming again and numb myself to prevent feeling pain. But to numb yourself from pain will cause you to numb yourself to feeling joy as well. Nonetheless, I have at last discovered that suppressing my emotions was deteriorating my soul. Thus, I allowed my true-self to let loose, and I'm still in the process of searching out the reasons behind every thought, belief, behavior, and emotion.

During this class quarter, I have taken the time to sit back and think: Am I this kind of person? Why do I do these types of actions? How do I truly feel about a specific subject or situation? And how do I want my life to be like in the future? Overall, I have learned that I do have a lot to say—only when I do not feel restricted or pressured to write within a specific format. The key to my writing, I believe, is to make it personal. Well, at least in my case. I have to care about what I want to say and write about because I want my readers to understand my genuineness. Moreover, I have learned to elaborate a whole lot more and not be so vague with my loaded ideas. I have learned to be proud of my work. I am going to keep most of the college papers that I have written to explain and express myself better to other people if they ask what I think. To tell you the truth, I wrote more for myself than for the English class itself - that is why my papers were so long.

Another factor that helped me improve my writing and improve my self-esteem has to do a lot with the use of a computer to print out my essays. I was finally able to turn in a paper without thousand white-out blotches decorating the front, as before, when I only had a typewriter at home.

In conclusion, I want to thank you, teacher, for being so understanding and relaxed when grading our assigned papers. I also want to thank you for making me feel comfortable enough to write as much as I needed to write to get a lot of stuff off my chest. It is real teachers like you that are the reasons why I now enjoy writing and expressing myself to the outside world without fear of failure.

The Genesis of Deep Circles

The Principal of Lee Mathson Middle School asked me if I'd be willing to do an intervention group for the highest risk 8th graders on campus? She explained that I had established good rapport with the students and they would ask about me often - when I was returning to campus? I remember taking a friend of mine to visit my mentees at Lee Mathson Middle and he said, "Are they out on recess?" And I responded, "Nope, they are just out of class, hanging out - cutting class."

He was shocked at how nonchalant this chronic "blah" culture was on campus. Anyways, back to my conversation with the Principal, I told her yes, but I would have to run the group after school because I had a full time job still and I was mentoring these teens as a volunteer on my spare time. She agreed. I had learned from my previous experience running groups - that the best way to set up the chairs was in a circle, so everybody is in the front row. After doing some team building activities, we got down to a self-awareness activity. I shared a list of reasons and motivations why people join gangs and the

82

reasons that keep them involved in gangs. I explained that I had compiled this list by asking myself, "Why I got involved in the first place? What motivated me for reals?"

I also added to the list the answers I heard from my childhood friends and dozens of other individuals (young and old) that I had interviewed in the past and I invited my group to identify their own motivators. After a few classes, the kids told me, "These Circle classes are Deep." Hence the name was born, "Deep Circles."

With Deep Circles, I free flow topics based on input from the students sitting around me. Each Deep Circle group was unique, because the key ingredients to this healing and paradigm shift eis the personal sharing. I always led by example and going deep first and sharing my own personal highs and lows, successes and failures, and traumas.

Ultimately, when new students would ask questions to determine if I was qualified enough to do gang intervention, or drug addiction intervention, or any other high risk life style intervention, my answer would circle back to this fact: "I cannot relate to everything you've been through. I cannot pretend to know what you've experienced. But I can relate to you as a human being who listens deeply so I can deeply understand you better. So, I am not qualified to have all the right answers, but I am qualified to ask all the right questions."

I tried everything to help these middle schoolers choose a different path. The last day of program, I showed the movie: "American Me" and at the end of the movie, only one mentee walked up to me and said, "I get it now. Thank you for saving my life." And from that point forward, she never turned back to that life style. She tried to help her friends, but neither I nor she was their medicine. It's always heart breaking when so many youngsters choose to learn the hard way and life becomes the teacher. But that first year, in listening to all of the deep sharing, I learned there's always I reason why a young life chooses to hang, bang, or slang, as Father Greg Boyle teaches.

I also learned that depression hides behinds many faces—anger, sadness, and even a smile. A mentee once told me, "I smile a lot, because nobody asks me what's wrong." Yet, we cannot heal from our past traumatic wounds until we feel safe and not judged. Scared Straight also doesn't work, because - You cannot scare somebody into caring about themselves.

Which are your motivators in life? If you are doing anything that is risky to your health and your future and can put you in jail, dead, or in the hospital, now is the time to ask yourself "Why?"

o   Painful Loneliness = Better gang friends, than to be a loner and have no friends.

o   Generational inheritance = My family and relatives were gang members before I was even born, so that's all I know.

o   Identity = I believe I am or was born a "gang member", and my street nickname because my permanent identity, which becomes a self-fulfilling prophesy

o   Self-Esteem = I feel pride that my gang is the toughest, biggest, or coolest. Especially when I can't feel proud about my athletic abilities, I don't know how it feels to win in sports, and I'm not proud of my academic grades yet.

- o   Attention = I Need to be seen and heard. When I wasn't involved in gangs, I was invisible, and so negative attention is better than no attention at all.
- o   Addicted to the Adrenaline Rush = Chasing the high of adrenaline from doing gang activity and crime.
- o   Debt & Loyalty = My gang friends helping me in the past, saving my life from an attack, I vowed to "owe them those favors" in gratitude.
- o   Protection = Fear bullies, walking the streets alone, with no back-up to help survive in the concrete jungle.
- o   Replacement "Family" bond = I feel closer to my gang friends than to my real/blood family. Or I'm an only child, so it feels good to call my friends: "Cousins", "brothers"
- o   Purpose = I want my death to mean something bigger than me, to die a heroic death like in the movies.
- o   Childhood Abuse = I get to punish others and make others feel the pain I felt or still feel. Misery loves company.
- o   Escape = I rather stay in the streets than to go home, because of the domestic violence, alcoholism, oppression, judgment, abuse at home.
- o   Boredom = The gang lifestyle is exciting, with more "stories" to brag about and show off, when I tell war-stories or almost-stories about: parties, police, fights, crime.
- o   More sex = Girls are attracted to the "bad boy". So, guys access to gang "groopies".

o   Usefulness = I feel important, like I can help in some way, even if I'm overweight or young, I can serve as a "look out", etc.

o   Revenge = I joined a gang or stay in a gang to keep hurting those who hurt me first.

o   Suicide = I don't want to live anymore, and would rather someone kill me. I have a death wish.

o   Reputation = I worked hard to "earn" my street cred.

o   Despair = I truly believe I can't change. It's too late to live a "normie" life.

o   Fear of Unknown = Starting over is way scarier. I know what to do and not do here.

o   Fear of Retaliation = If I try to leave, my "friends" will kill me.

o   Fast Money

o   I'm Lost = I don't know why. I'm just following blindly.

o   To achieve manhood = to be respected as a man, to feel tough and strong.

o   Co-dependency = I hate those that my boyfriend hate. I hate those that my friends hate. I hate those that my older siblings hate.

o   Power to Control = I like feeling the power to control a street, a park, and the power to intimidate others and make them fear me.

Writing exercise 15: Describe the ideal guy or a girl you would like to fall in love with to marry one day in the future? Do you know what you're looking for? What would be the three deal-breakers that you should never tolerate?

Knowledge

Quote:

"Education is what helps you to:
See more when you look,
Hear more when you listen,
Ponder deeper when you think, and
See more when you speak!" —**Unknown**

There are three levels of knowledge and learning:

1.) The first level of knowledge is information. The stuff you know that you already know, for example, like your name or tying your shoe. You know you know your name and how to tie your shoe, right? Right.

2.) The second level of knowledge is information that you don't know. In other words, what you know, that you don't know. For example, I know that I don't know calculus math.

3.) The third level of knowledge is the hardest to understand, but the most important. In this level of expertise, it's not knowing or being aware of all the stuff you don't know. In college, I learned about things I never thought about and didn't even know existed. But, it's going to be tough mentally, because you will have to leave your old way of thinking behind, and instead keep your mind blank. Your brain open to the words and ideas in each class but also to my writings as well because it is in this third level of knowledge that authentic learning happens.

It is like going to Mexico for the first time. You have to leave your United States mentality in the luggage, because me knowing the number to pizza delivers, is not going to help me in a Ranchito in Mexico when I'm hungry. A better example isí the English language itself. When you are in Mexico, talking to your *abuelita, tíos, and tías* in English will not be useful to communicate. So, my point is, once you step out of your comfort zone, you will begin to expand your mind. Same with teachers, principals, or counselors.

When they see F's on a report card, they assume the young person needs more academic tutoring. But in reality, F grades on a report card simply tells me there's a problem and the student does not care enough about their own future to ask for help. Same with gang involvement or using drugs or cutting arms or running away, etc. Those are simply clues that there's a deeper problem somewhere else. Let's look at it this way. How do you know you have mice inside a building? Usually by what's obvious, by what can be seen—the mice droppings. But the problem isn't the mice poop and the solution is not cleaning it up. The mouse droppings is simply the evidence that you have mice in the building. And once you heal that mouse/trauma, guess what?

The "problems" (ie: F grades, truancy, fighting, drug/ alcohol use, gang activity, unprotected sex, crime, etc) all of it, will go away automatically. I've had mentees stop doing self-destructive behaviors by never talking about those behaviors, but instead digging deeper on the root cause of the anger, sadness, etc. Usually it goes like this—every child has a dream, likes school, and smiles and laughs and plays all the time - until something happens. Ask yourself, "When did things start going downhill?" And the young person will usually look sad, before they tell you what grade or what age the event happened.

Writing exercise 16: If you had three wishes, what would you wish for and why? But, you cannot wish for money, a big house, a new car, or more wishes. Lol.

Jan. 28th, 2003

The University's Resident-Cholo

When I got to Santa Clara University, I thought to myself, "Let's see how long I last before I get kicked out." I didn't know I could make it through college, because I would hear "A students" telling me that college was stressful for them, and that made me lose faith because I've always been a C+ average student. However, to my surprise, when I got my first "A" grade at a university-level English class, I knew I earned it because nobody knew to be here.

Back at Bellarmine, I believed the only reason I got passing grades was that teachers felt sorry for me or because they thought too fondly of me to give me a bad grade. But, when I saw an "A" on my SCU report card, I was happy. I told random people that "I've never seen an A before in my life!" After that day, I walked around the SCU campus, thinking to myself: "I belong here I'm not transferring nowhere! Even if it takes me six years, I'm going to graduate from Santa Clara University! I'll only worry about one class at a time. I'll get there, slowly, but surely!"

A few weeks later, the financial aid office told me I had extra money from school grants that I had not used yet. So, I asked them if I could use it to live on campus in a dorm room? And they said yes. However, I told them I wanted a single place. And when they asked why? I told them three reasons:

1.)   Because I didn't get along with males since I had a bad temper. Mainly because I didn't tolerate any disrespect or perceived disrespect.

2.)   I was homophobic, meaning that I didn't want to sleep or get dressed in the same room with another dude doing the same.

3.)   Lastly, I told them I have frequent violent nightmares that caused me to swing and kick in my sleep. I didn't think it would be safe for my roommate, especially a male roommate, but I was okay with a female roommate, Lol.

Using their common sense, they said okay and agreed because they saw the serious look on the face that I wasn't lying about the fact that I would indeed fuck a fool up if they tried to get brave or stupid with me. Especially if I had female company over.

So, my first night staying in the dorms, I decided to go to the cafeteria to have dinner like all the other students who lived on-campus. When I walked into the dining hall, I immediately heard: clink-clink-clink-clink-clink-clink-clink-clink-clink-clink-clink-clink-clink-clink-clink-clink. Which were the sound of over one-hundred spoons and forks tapping the plates when every student in the cafeteria stopped eating at the same time. The entire room got quiet. As I walked towards the far wall of the cafeteria to select my food, I could feel over

200 eyes looking at me, feeling super awkward as I walked through the fog of eerie silence. When I got in line with my empty plate, one of the kitchen managers walked directly up to me and asked me: "May I help you?" (Obviously, he thought I was lost and or was trespassing and didn't belong here).

But I responded politely, "No, I go here."

After I got my food, I sat down at an empty table. Each table was round in shape and had ten chairs around it. I noticed the place was packed, but students were still coming in to get their food. But I also noticed that nobody approached my table even though there were nine empty chairs.

White people the packed whole place. It felt like another Bellarmine campus, except there were females here. I then noticed a table with a bunch of Latina sitting there, eating. And I thought to myself, when they are done eating, I'm sure they'll come over to say hi because they must know how I'm feeling. Like a single pinto bean, and a huge bag of white rice. But, when they finished eating, they walked right past me.

They didn't even look at me; just ignored me. And I got hell a mad! (On the inside). I was mumbling to myself, saying: "Fuck those bitches, fucking sellouts! I expected that type of treatment from all these white people, to be ignored, but not for my own Raza. So, from that day on, I told myself I would ignore everybody the way they ignored me. When I saw any Latinos on campus, I would say in my head: "Fuck these coconuts!" I no longer cared what anybody at that school thought of me. So, I continue to dress and do whatever I felt like doing. If I felt like walking out of class, I did. I was the only one on campus walking around in my tank tops, cut off's, white knee socks, wino slippers, beanies, locs shades, Pendleton's, etc. I also started inviting all my homeboys to come to kick back with me at SCU. I would drive up to campus bumping my beats, with a carload of homeboys, who were all tatted-down on their heads, necks, sleeves, to hang out, lift weights, eat in the cafeteria, play pool, or just lounge with hynas (rucas) we would bring over to mess with.

One day, I overheard my homeboy say to a girl on the phone: "I'm at Santa Clara University. My homeboy Silent goes here. One of us made it."

So, even as a college student, my homeboys still saw me as one of them. Which felt good. Because I always worried about being thought of as a sellout for choosing a school. It was tough for me to be away from my homeboys for so many years while I was in classes all day than in libraries for hours and hours doing homework. I felt guilty of not being around to help them maintain the hood.

That year, I relapse back into my old gang member identity. Silent came back to my life. I became more paranoid, angry, and sexually active. I brought all kinds of girls to my dorm room-which I called my personal "mo-mo." It got to the point where I heard my reputation at SCU was of me being with a different girl every week. But I didn't care what SCU thought.

To illustrate my point, I would walk into class with a knife on my belt, displayed. Never concealed. Nobody ever said anything. Not even the teachers. But hanging around my homeboys, driving around the streets with them—my face got out there more; so, I had to worry about my safety, since I associated with active gang homeboys. I got so paranoid that I felt I had to carry a .22 loaded pistol in my car, and I also kept it in my dorm room. In truth, every time anybody knocked on my door, I looked through the peep-hole, with the gun in my hand ready. I actually wrote my will that year and pushed myself to finish the first draft of this book to see a complete before I died.

No matter what my homeboys were involved in, only around my homeboys did I ever feel completely accepted just the way I am. They never looked at me like a strange zoo animal the way I felt SCU people saw me.

I enjoyed laughing with my Homies that Freshman year. Then they all got locked up later that year. I felt lonely again. So, I began calling all my ex-"girlfriends" to come over and keep me company. And I tried my best to please their bodies so they would come back again.

For the first two years at SCU, I worked full-time. So, besides taking three classes, which made me a full-time student, and about thirty hours of homework every week. I also worked full-time, which was forty hours a week as a security guard. This is considered a "Full-Time, Full-Time Student." Meaning that I would get off of work at 1 am in the morning, go back to the dorms, take a shower, go to sleep, then be in class by 8 am every day, Monday through Friday.

So, I would get about five hours of sleep every night. But frequently, a female bedroom buddy would sleepover and going fifteen rounds per night, so I hardly got any sleep. Due to the lack of sleep and action-packed daily schedule, the first year, I was a stress case. I was successfully juggling a full-time girlfriend, a few *sanchas* sprinkled in, hanging full-time with homeboys, a full-time job, a full schedule classes with tons of homework. Plus I would lift weights twice a week, not to mention spending time with my family, plus maybe eat three meals per day; so, I knew I had to cut back on trying to be all things for all people, for my sanity.

At SCU, when the summer hits, all the students living on campus had to move out of the dorms. Everybody was always super excited and happy to go home finally. I was too. But a couple of weeks before I was supposed to move back home, my dad told me rival gang members were coming to our apartment looking for me, calling me out, and waiting outside for me. So, my dad said for me to find a room to rent somewhere else during the summer. But I didn't listen. I missed my parents and my home.

So, I packed up my room at SCU and loaded the boxes into my white Pontiac, and drove back home. However, when I drove up to my street, I noticed a couple of rivals walking by, and they saw me. I parked my car, grabbed a box of my belongings, and carried my things inside my parent's apartment. My mom always had a hot plate of food ready for me to eat when she knows I'm on my way. After greeting my parents with hugs, I told them I had to get a few more boxes from my car. And because of street smarts habit, I looked out the window before going outside. When I looked down at the sidewalk, two of my rivals were standing outside, waiting for me. I had heard through the grapevine that one of them was packing a gun and flashed it to a neighbor boy around the block. So, I didn't want to go out there, unarmed. So the internal struggle started within me.

One side of me wanted to go out there and handle some business. But the other part of me didn't want my parents to see it happen. I thought about calling the homeboys, but then I remembered that they were all locked up. So, my anger side won, and I started walking down the stairs to rush these two fools. My mom recognized the look on my face and knew what I was about to do, so she followed me down the steps and pleaded with me, "¡M'ijo! No salgas! ¡Déjalos m'ijo!"

As soon as I opened the front door, my mom yelled out to my dad in desperation, "¡Va para afuera!" My dad then appeared at the top of the stairs with the phone to his ear and said to me, "Le estoy llamando a la policía." And he walked out of view, and I heard him talking on the phone. At that point, I decided to close the door because I knew my mom would follow me outside, and I didn't want to put her in danger either.

Protecting my family was always my top priority, above my ego or anger. So, I sat at the bottom of the steps to wait, with my box next to me. I knew what was going to happen next. Any moment, I would hear the sound of loud banging on the door. *BANG! BANG! BANG! BANG!* "SAN JOSE POLICE DEPARTMENT!!" I explained to the lady cop what had happened, pointing at my box as evidence that I was telling the truth.

The lady cop asked my dad, "So, what's the solution?"

And my dad responded that he believed I wasn't safe being at home.

So, the police officer looked at me sternly and said to me, "You heard him. Get your stuff. I'll stand by while you put your box back in your car. You have 5 minutes"

Walking outside, escorted by the police officer, was the walk of shame. I overheard on the police radio report that another cop car had chased the rivals down the street somewhere. My mom looked sad, and my dad looked relieved. I looked pissed, but not at my dad. I understood his reason for having me leave.

I was angry at those rivals for sabotaging my return home, which lasted ten minutes. I drove to Santa Clara; it was already late. I looked for a quiet street. I parked next to a fence and sat there in disbelief. When it got dark, I climbed to the back seat of my car, I took off my tennis shoes, and I wrapped my hooded sweater around my shoes to serve as my comfy pillow that night, sleeping in my car. I slept in my car for two nights until I found a room for rent nearby.

That summer, I was forced to live alone in a place I rented in the city of Santa Clara. I stayed away from my parents because I realized the sad fact that my family is safer with me, not around. I was angry and bitter. Sorry when I would hear my mom say to me: *"No vengas para este lado m'ijo."* And then I would get angry when I thought about why I couldn't go home. So, that summer, I asked my homies to borrow a gun.

(Deep down, I was glad I did not have a gun earlier, because I would have been tempted to go out there blasting.)

During my second year at SCU, I kept busy lifting weights and having sex. My weight lifting partner told me that students at SCU referred to me as "The gangster of SWIG." (SWIG was the name of the dorm building I live in for two years.) It's the tallest dorm building on the Santa Clara University campus, which is eleven stories high. In a letter that my homeboy Bones wrote to me, he said: "I can see your building (SWIG) from my building when I look at the window here at the Main Jail." He went on to reflect that he wished he could be the bird he saw outside free. He reflected further that we both grew up in the same neighborhood (two streets away actually), we went to the same middle school. But we chose two different paths, which led to two different places—opposite extremes actually.

Back to me living at SWIG Hall - given that it is the tallest building on campus (eleven floors high), all of us students who live there, always had to wait about 10 minutes for the elevator to come back down. There were only two elevators for over 1000 student residents. Given this limit, as soon as the elevator doors opened, about twelve people rush in and squeeze in there, to avoid waiting another ten minutes.

One day, I walked into the lobby with a female friend. I saw about eighteen other students waiting for the elevator as well. So, when the elevator door open, my female visitor and I walked in, and we notice, and nobody else got in. Those other eighteen SCU students just stood there, none of them brave enough to get in the elevator with us —preferring to wait another ten minutes. We both were cracking up with laughter the whole way up.

But that's not the worst type of racism I've experienced at SCU. The worst is when I still get asked: "How did you get into Santa Clara?" Everybody asks me that question, as soon as they find out that I attend SCU. But let me ask you: how am I supposed to answer that question? It's almost like they are expecting me to say I snuck in through the back door or a window. It's not okay for people to ask you: "How did you get into Bellarmine or Santa Clara University." Because, how many white people get asked that same question? None.

When people look at me, they see a hoodlum. It doesn't matter how I dress like, because when cops pulled me over, all they can see is from my chest up when I'm driving in my car. I've been profiled and pulled over multiple times - all because I was DWBAB: Driving While Brown And Bald.

But I don't regret looking the way I do. I don't regret going to SCU. Because my purpose at SCU was to infiltrate, then agitate. Because it's okay to make people uncomfortable until everybody gets used to seeing more and more bald cholos at universities and inside the classroom, not just mowing the campus lawn. *"Porque aquí estoy, y no me voy."* —Grito Serpentino.

If people don't like it, they can transfer out. It's our turn. Our time. Fill up the classrooms! Not the prisons.

Quotes:

- *"No one can make you feel inferior without your consent."* —Eleanor Roosevelt
- *"Luck is what happens when preparation meets opportunity."* —Seneca
- *"I've learned that opportunities are never lost; someone will take the ones you miss."* —Andy Rooney

In closing, here is the wisdom nugget. Do more than just enrolling in college. Do more than just showing up to all your classes. Do more than just memorizing what the professor says or what the book teaches. Do more than understanding why you are learning those facts. Do more than be able to teach what you learned to others. Because the ultimate "Do more" is not simply to learn and become more intelligent. Because being smart, being intelligent, and even being a genius, is not more than being wise. And reaching wisdom is evident when you are able to put into practice and apply what you've learned into your real life to make your life better and help make the lives better of those in your family, friends circle, neighborhood, and beyond.

In other words, you can't get rid of bad habits until you replace those habits with better, safer, healthier people, thoughts, feelings, and actions. And if you don't know how to start, the beginning of all wisdom is to know you don't know enough—so seek out wise counsel. Scan your life for adults who are at least five years older than you and have achieved something you want to achieve. Do you want to buy a house one day? Then find a mentor that owns a house. Do you want to graduate from college? Then find a mentor who graduated from college already? Do you want to have a career that pays over $100k? Then find a mentor who is already doing that. Do you want to become a police officer? Teacher? Business owner? Then guess who you should have as a mentor? And once you identify who those people are, then decide to be bold enough to ask them to be your official mentors and then have the common sense to follow all their advice.

Writing exercise 17: If you knew you were going to die in seven days, what would you do in those last seven days? Make a list of at least twenty things or more.

Chapter 5

Forgive Me

Please forgive me Tata-Dios - Do not assault,
I have sinned - it's my fault;

I'm sorry for what I *did* today,
I know it is sinful in your eyes - not OK;

I'm sorry for what I failed to do today,
I was not in tune with you in anyway;

I'm sorry for the bad words that I used today,
I need to watch what I say;

I'm sorry for that evil thought in my mind today,
I will pray;

Please Forgive Me - this message I send,
Because I have fallen again;

I ask you for your forgiveness once more,
because I want to keep trying - do not shut the door.

I want you to be proud of me,
give me time - you'll see.

But, I remember you said:
 "Get this through your head!

<u>Trying</u> to do good and <u>wanting</u> to do good,
<u>Is</u> what's right—understood?

Because when my soul feels weak like this - sad,
you are not mad.

Instead, it is <u>Now</u> that I am strong,
because I know I am wrong.

And I need you to heal me.
Please Forgive me.

Writing exercise 18: Can you relate to the author in any way thus far? If yes, which life experiences, which thoughts, which feelings?

Loneliness, and the Search for Love and to be Loved Back

When I live by myself in the college dorms, I would lay on my bed and wish for someone to be there next to me. I longed for a kind female's company, not just for sex, but to hug and hold, who would make me feel loved and cared for. But most times, nobody was there. I had no high school sweetheart (since I went to an all-boys high school), and I never had a significant long-term relationship that lasted more than three months. However, the more I thought of it, the sadder I became - feeling sorry for myself. I would say to myself, nobody loves me. But, no matter what I tried, the only thing that made me feel better was talking about it out loud, even if I was all alone laying on my bed at night—letting it all out. Giving all the tears of agony flow out, and drip onto my pillow and wiping them off with the sleeve of my sweater.

This was helpful because it made me feel human. I say this because, during my entire middle school years and high school years, I was unable to cry physically. I even tried yawning a whole bunch just to make sure my tear ducts still worked. Maybe I couldn't cry because I had too much hate in my heart and because I believed it was a weak act, thus I refused.

Only after I pushed past the pain, and swam across the cold lake of loneliness, I discovered something valuable on the other shore—solitude. The difference between loneliness and solitude is that loneliness is painful, and solitude is peaceful. Ever since I arrived at the shores of solitude, I have never felt lonely ever again. I am totally fine by myself. I no longer need anybody to be okay. My loved ones are bonus blessings for me to love and enjoy our time together.

But if you are still swimming in the frigid waters or on the loneliness shore afraid to feel that feelings again, I invite you to think about it this way. If you do not have a significant other right now in your life, I believe your future mate is fixing him/her up right now for the day to finally meet. Think about it this way, you don't want to meet your future mate while they are all bitter after a break-up or still immature, right? Then be patient and in the meantime, work on fixing yourself up, so that you will be ready for him/or her, when the destined time comes.

Here's my theory: I believe the heart, your heart, my soul, is like a plant. All the plant (your heart) wants is to be fed water/love. And the plant/heart, does not care who waters/loves it. The heart just wants to feel loved. But what if somebody walks by the plants and spits on the plan?, Or pours beer on the plant?, Or pees on the plan? He/or she is watering the plant, right? Yes, they are. But he/or she is also disrespecting the plant's worth.

Have you ever heard that saying: love is blind? Because it's true. The heart, your heart, and my heart is blind and will cling on to anybody who spits, pees, or pours beer on it. The heart doesn't mind getting negative attention, as long as it's getting some type of attention/moisture.

So, that is why it is so important to use your brain to select a good person. Don't allow your heart to decide, because most of us have a starving heart and is impatient and will settle. Keep your heart in check.

One morning, in 10th grade, a priest/ mentor of mine was driving me to the Day Worker Center, where I used to do volunteer hours teaching ESL. During the drive, I had told him that I wanted to become a priest. With a caring tone of voice, he asked me, "Why?" I told him, well, I know the world is going to end, and there's is only two places you can go after we die - heaven or hell. And hell, is not a very lovely place to end up. And the priest asked me, "What if there was a better place than heaven?" And that response stumped me. I was stuck. I had never considered that option. Then he said, "You see Enrique, you have to want to go to heaven, because you love heaven, not because you think it's a better place." And I tried to relate that to my future soul mate. There's always going to be somebody more beautiful, more intelligent, more giving, yet the same question remains: "Do you love her because she's beautiful? Or is she beautiful because you love her?"

Quote:
"To laugh is to risk appearing a fool,
To weep is to risk appearing sentimental,
To reach out to another is to risk involvement,

To expose feelings is to risk exposing your true self,

To place your ideas and dreams before a crowd is to risk their loss,

To love is to risk not being loved in return,

To live is to risk dying,

To hope is to risk despair,

To try is to risk failure,

But risks must be taken because the greatest hazard in life is to risk nothing,

He may avoid suffering and sorrow,

But he cannot learn, feel, change, grow, or live,

Chained by his servitude, he is a slave who has forfeited all freedom,

Only a person who risks is free." —Leo F. Buscaglia

Writing exercise 19: When is the last time you cried? What happened that caused you to flow tears of pain?

Chapter 6

The New Beginning

Growing up, starting around age fifteen, I was looking for guidance. I was looking for answers. I didn't know what the purpose of my life was, like why I was even born. My parents always guilt-tripped me to join them to church every single Sunday, whether I felt like going or not. But, truthfully, going to church never really help me when I was growing up, because I was always too busy checking out all the fine girls and also distracted by every door, scanning for rivals or any potential threat that might walk in.

But, I heard the Bible had all the answers, so I decided to find out for myself. We didn't own a copy in my house. The only Bible my dad had was an old one that was written in Spanish, with some red color sentences written in Latin. So, I didn't read it because I couldn't understand the vocabulary in Spanish. So, what I decided to do was to find a Bible. I called bookstores to see how much one cost. I chose instead to ask somebody who already had one to borrow it.

I was surprised that a white guy from my school gave me his old Bible, one with the Old Testament and the New Testament. Then, a couple of months later, my counselor gave me a brand new one that only had the New Testament. Honestly, the reason why I wanted to find the Bible so badly was that my soul was thirsty for something like that. Something good, something that would understand me, something that would teach me how to be a good person.

I would never invite homeboys to go to church with me; I would just go alone. As first because my parents dragged me as a teen, but then as I got older, I went on my own because once in a while, a priest would say something interesting or comforting that made me think. This one time, a homeboy of mine asked me if I would take them to church? And I did, but he would only go if I give him a ride. And the way I see it, if you need or want something bad enough, you'd go no matter what.

I learned over time that it's not helpful to carry somebody who can walk. For example, I've read the entire Bible over four times already. I highlighted a bunch, then re-read over my highlights, and underlined more stuff. I also watched the movie "Jesus of Nazareth" at least five times as well. It taught me that today is a new day, a new beginning. It's not where you're from; it's where you're at, and where you are going that count. Who you were yesterday doesn't exist anymore. Who are you today? And who do you want to become tomorrow?

Quote:

"Each night, when I go to sleep, I die. And the next morning, when I wake up, I am reborn."—Mahatma Gandhi

If someone were to ask me, "How do I start changing?" or

114

"How do I get my student/son/daughter/brother/sister to change?"

I would honestly recommend they read my memoir: *Barrio Side Hero*, published in 2019 by Floricanto Press. It's truly an intervention tool that I've assigned to mentees to read and then they talk about their thoughts, feelings, and feedback.

Writing exercise 20: What do you believe happens after you die? If you believe in Heaven, describe it. What do you think is the purpose of your life? Do you believe you have a calling? To achieve here on earth?

God

I was in a philosophy class one time, and the professor gave us the final exam question that stumps us all. All of us students asked out loud, how can that be possible? The problem was: "Explain how God can know the past, present, future, right now, right at this very second, all at the same time?"

As part of the final exam, we had to each write an essay on how that was possible. Some in my study-group asked, "If God knows what's going to happen in the future, then what's the point of paying for something to change?" I have to admit, it took me a long time to finally make sense of it. We were all sitting in a study group when I came up with this explanation:

"Okay, imagine we are walking on the sand at the beach. Imagine God is looking down at us. Now, by our footprints, God knows where we've been, he knows all of our personal histories. And he knows exactly where in our life journey we are at right now. But God does not control us like mere puppets on strings.

God made us with the free-will to do whatever we choose. And God gave us an infinite number of choices. However, God knows the results and consequences of every one of those options. He knows exactly what is going to happen if you choose path A, path B, path C, etc. But it's up to us. And if we pray and humbly ask for his help, God will guide us and drop a few hints along the trails that lead to some hidden opportunities behind disguised doors.

Spirituality with God

I've learned that we all define our higher power differently, such as:

1.) A "Fun God" —who says: "If it feels good, do it; so party till you die.

2.) A "Punisher God" —who is all about fairness and believes "Karma's a bitch!"

3.) A "Mountain God" —believing that the Creator created the world, then left (far up to the Mountain); and, either: a.) seize the world from high above like watching TV for entertainment purposes, or b.) does not even care to know what is going on in our lives. However, either way, it is still absent.

4.) Lastly, I consider God a Loving God - who cares about us and our lives and gets involved with affection and forgiveness as a close-close friend.

5.) Sadly, I often treat God as a "Spare-Tire God," which means I seek God's help when trouble arises; and when things get better, I put God back in the trunk and forget about my Great Mentor once again.

Quote:
"I believe in the sun - even when it is night;
I believe in love - even when I am alone;
I believe in God - even when he is silent."

Writing exercise 21: Who is your hero or heroine? Who or where do you look up to for advice or guidance? Who is that person? And what have they taught you? Do you follow their advice?

Chapter 7

Philosophy/Metaphysics

Feb. 18th, 2001

Life According to A, B, or C

Sociology

It is important to admit that limits to existing in this world. We are born into a certain economic class and a particular race with a specific language that constructs our reality and how we define and see the world. For example, let's say a person is born in a desert area in Africa, and his or her parents and the rest of the population living in that remote and isolated desert, have never seen snow before (not even on TV or in a magazine). So, that community of people probably will not have a word in their language to describe snow or hail, given that they have never seen or touched it before. Hence, the concept of snow does not exist to them, because it is not a part of their world; that is their knowledge.

To use a more personal example: growing up, I believe that the only way to go to college was if my family had thousands of dollars to send me to college. So, I had given up on the idea. But, when I was in my junior year in high school,

I was taught/educated/made aware that something called "financial aid" existed. But, I was skeptical, so I asked, "Let me get this right: the poorer I am, the more money they give me? How does that work?" So, I continued to ask more questions to find more answers. Thus limited options exist, but through education, you expand your knowledge of what's available and how to get there, to expand your options, and enlarge your world ultimately.

My Life

I firmly believe I am in the process of heading towards my life destiny. And I define destiny - as the main "plan," the purpose for my existence, according to God. I argue that I, or anyone, can do this also, by following their gut-instinct/little voice. But how do you know which voice to listen? Because there are so many options available to us in our everyday world, like, whether to speed up or slow down when the light turns yellow. I accomplish this by trusting my conscience because by stopping at a red light, that moment's decision could have prevented me from running over a child running into the street-chasing a ball, because such an occurrence is based on timing. But again, how do you know it is your conscience that you are trusting?

Well, I describe and identify the little voice in the following manner. For example, if somebody tells you to guess a number between one and 10. And the very first number that pops into your head is seven. Then what? Do you say that number? But it's so quick, like a flash, that you say to yourself, "Well, I didn't really choose the number 7." So, you start doubting your own gut instinct, and argue with yourself silently, thinking seven is too obvious, everybody knows "lucky number seven", so maybe it's four, or maybe it's 10, or maybe it's two?

So you put your confidence in your logic (conscious) self, instead of trusting in God who talks to you through your deeper conscience/that little voice in your subconscious. But most of us trust in ourselves more than God, so we guess wrong, and when the person says, it was seven, you yell out "I was going to say that!" So, if you are wise, you would have instead of gone back to the original number given/reveal to you and trust your Conscience a.k.a. God. But, just to clarify, following your gut instinct does not mean you do things that feels easy or comfortable, because some of the best things in life can only be achieved through a lot of struggle and feeling uncomfortable while doing something new.

To tell my story and why I believe I have a mission in life: I believe everybody has a mission in life with no role being too small or insignificant. The truth is those people behind the scenes are the ones that help us the most by providing bridges use to cross over to greener pastures. I can track my destiny since my birth, but I recently realized it more clearly during my late teens as I reflected back on my life. Because each life experiences (good or bad, job I loved or job I hates) served like a step on a ladder that allowed me to reach the next rung.

A.)   I was born December 3, but to get into kindergarten at that time, you had to be born on or before

December 2. Initially, this seems like bad luck, a negative, but I will demonstrate how this set back was actually a blessing in disguise.

B.)   My mom went and argued with the school teacher, principal, and school district for months in order to get me into school, but she did not succeed. I believe I was meant to wait one year to start school because my mom tried to the best of her ability.

C.)   Using my logic and imagination, I believe that if I would have been in school one year ahead, I would have went into the same high school and during the same time that my older brother attended Overfelt High School, exactly one school year before the district changed its boundaries. And this is significant, because my brother belongs to a gang back in those days, and I would have joined his gang as soon as possible.

D.)   But, because I was born one day later and I was forced to be held back from school one entire year, my gang initiation day was postponed one year, because I didn't attend gang meetings with my brother until I was in 7th grade.

E.)   As a result of his postpone meeting, I did not end up joining the street gang. By divine intervention, my brother got stabbed two weeks before my scheduled gang initiation. But because of my brother's natural consequence for gang involvement, I had the chance to do a cost/benefit analysis and decided I would be safer not being under the control of a gang as an official member, but instead, just to hang around and associate with gang members because I will still have the freedom to come and go as I pleased, with some degree of protection aka "back up."

F.)   And I firmly believe that if I would have been born a day sooner, I would have definitely joined my brothers' gang before he got stabbed, and without a doubt, I would have been actively involved in various gang banging activities to the fullest, leading to life in prison for murder because I had the desire to prove myself.

G.)   That is why I do not believe in coincidences or accidents anymore, because I believe I was stabbed in the 8th grade for a higher purpose, which sounds weird I know. I say that getting physically injured can part of destiny's intervention, because it pushed me towards a different path. I call these "push blessings". After getting stabbed in 8th grade, I refuse to go to Independence High School where all my enemies felt emboldened. If it were up to me, I would have chosen to go to Overfelt High School where my brother was already getting a click of homeboys to look out for me.

H.)   My dad was a chef/cook at a restaurant for many years. He enjoyed his work very much. But destiny took place again when my dad's employers had to close down the restaurant. Thus, my father was forced to look for other work immediately, since we needed to pay the rent or become homeless. Which landed him getting employed at Santa Clara University as a janitor. This job allowed my father to hear about the high school nearby called Santa Clara High. So, when I told him it was not a good idea for me to attend Independence

High School, he was able to provide another option that he was made aware existed.

I.)   However, the district did not give us permission to transfer. So, my family exercised our free will, and my brother and I (both still teenagers) went to the Santa Clara High School office and lied to them and said we were given permission by the district to transfer and they allowed me to enroll.

J.)   Now let's compare this admission process "challenge" between my 9th grade year and kindergarten year. I was not allowed into kindergarten despite my mom's relentless efforts for four straight months, but on the other hand, I was allowed into Santa Clara High not by a parent, but by my gang member-looking teenage brother, with a lie.

K.)   Another example is my father getting a job as a janitor at Santa Clara University, joining a team of over 100 janitors on the massive campus. However, my dad was the only janitor out of all the SCU janitors to get promoted at work in the building where the influential leaders of the University lived, the Jesuit Residence. As a result, the Jesuits made it possible for me to enter into Bellarmine College Preparatory, which was perfect timing, because I was beginning to hang out with more gang members at Santa Clara High and I also began cutting school and using drugs, as well as acquiring new enemies and became sexually active without protection; so I knew if I didn't leave Santa Clara High—I would have self-sabotaged my future in some way share or form.

L.) Lastly, destiny revealed itself by allowing my father to get hired just enough years at Santa Clara University for him to quality for their "tuition remission" program/ policy that allows full time employees with over four years of employment to have their children attend Santa Clara University free of charge, zero tuition. This is significant, because I know for a fact I would have refused to attend college if my parents had to attempt to pay college tuition, because I keenly aware of their/our financial struggles.

M.) So, I believe my dad is living according to his own destiny, by sacrificing himself in order to be my bridge, which will allow me to help my entire family and others, as a College Grad.

N.) After graduating from Santa Clara University, I got hired at Bellarmine College Prep of all places as the Diversity Outreach Director and Admissions Assistant Director to recruit more low income Latino students and guess where I went first to recruit? One East Side Project was never enough. I recruited and got in 50 in less than five years.

In short, I do not believe my life and my presence here at SCU and back at Bellarmine is a coincidence as a result of random accidents. And if I mess up in any way, I believe with confidence that there will be hidden detours, because God believes in 2nd, 3rd, 4th chances as long as we don't make it too difficult for God to get us out of our mess.

FREE WILL:

I believe we are a product of our environment "Autopilot mode", until we realize it; then, from that point on, we are on "Brain-on" mode and we can no longer use sociology's product of our environment, as an excuse. But, before you begin reaching for a positive goal, you need to be: 1.) optimistic - believe it can be done; 2.) Have self-confidence - I am the one who will do it!; and 3.) Be persistent in action—actually doing it!

Quote:

"There are three types of people in the world:
Those who Make things happen,
Those who Watch things been,
And those who Wonder what happened."—Mary Kay Ash

At age twenty-three, I decided to start my own non-profit organization called: "East Side Heroes". I had no clue how to start a business, but I did know that I wanted to replicate what was done for me, because it worked. I wanted to provide other young boys and girls with the following growth opportunities:

1.)   Academic Scholarships/financial aid to attend a private/college-prep high school.

2.)   Community Service projects helping animals, kids, the elderly, those with special needs, and the homeless because doing this type of volunteer hours helped bring my heart back to life to have compassion for all living things - aka human kindness.

3.)   Leadership skills by being put in charge of different projects and customer service verbal skills and gaining self-confidence with completing tasks.

4.)   Recruiting a team of 3-5 life-long mentors to surround each young mentee so that there's never reliance on just one support person and that wise advisor can help with different challenges at different stages in life.

Father Greg Boyle, Founder of "Jobs for a Future Nonprofit" one time told me, "We both do the same thing—except I use jobs and you use education to transform lives." And he was right, me working helped me stay busy and out of trouble and taught me self-confidence, leadership skills, and gave me access to tons of older co-worker mentors. I retired from East Side Heroes as the sole Founder after 13 years as a volunteer Executive Director. I didn't enjoying running a business. I only enjoyed teaching others how to mentor and the innovative community service projects. I described it this way—I am a chef who enjoys perfecting my craft/recipes.

I am not passionate about running a restaurant or expanding a franchise. I would design intervention projects/programs and place them on the shelf for a believer to come along and fund my ideas. One of those believers is my mentor Dave Cortese. One day he says to me, "If you could design any program and didn't have to worry about the funding, what would you do?" And 24 hours later, I presented him with "The Corazon Project" neighborhood transformation model.

128

He loved it. And I ran it successfully for 6 years until my health failed me. But the model proved successful year after year, with our "Deep Circles", "Murals with a Message," and "Unity Days."

News

San Jose neighborhood, long familiar to gang violence, celebrates a day of peace

Me, Enrique Flores, on the left and my childhood best friend, Rich, on the right side, who arrived at a "Unity Day" to show his support.

By John Boudreau | Mercury News, Bay Area News Group

PUBLISHED: March 24, 2012 at 1:26 p.m. | UPDATED: August 13, 2016 at 5:40 a.m.

Some brought their "colors" — red or blue shirts and caps symbolizing gang allegiances. Others showed up with knives and guns.

Saturday's gathering in East San Jose, though, wasn't a confrontation but a meeting on neutral ground — Most Holy Trinity Church. And the purpose was promoting peace amid the seemingly endless gang wars that torment neighborhoods and families in this part of the city.

Gang members and former members — and those whose lives have been touched by the violent feuds — were asked to bring in gang paraphernalia in exchange for gift cards and participate in a march through residential streets to promote peace.

"It's about identity transformation," said Enrique Flores, director of the Corazón Project, a nonprofit founded by Supervisor Dave Cortese. The youth project sponsored Unity Day II.

Flores, a Santa Clara University graduate who in his younger years was headed in the wrong direction, now mentors youths in an effort to steer them away from gangs.

The project focuses on the neighborhoods in the Welch Park or Overfelt High School area, a slice of the city particularly known for gang violence bounded by Ocala Avenue to the north, Tully Road to the south, King Road to the west and Capitol Expressway to the east.

A majority of the households in the area have been touched by gang violence over the years, Cortese said. "Now we are touching them with acts of nonviolence," he added.

The effort includes mentoring young people, who in turn become advocates to their peers for turning away from gangs, Cortese said. Started just a year ago, the project has already made a mark in the neighborhoods: Young people have painted murals promoting nonviolence throughout the area.

If the event, which attracted dozens of participants, was aimed at spotlighting an alternative to young people lured by gang life, it also underscored how many lives have been shattered by it.

Although Anthony Hernandez said he avoided getting involved in gangs, two of his friends were killed in separate shootings.

"This helps spread the word: Gang violence isn't right," said the twenty-year-old, clad in black. "I lost a couple of friends to gang violence. It didn't seem right, chasing a color, fighting."

The march through the streets began late in morning and lasted until about 1 p.m. Young people carried signs with slogans such as "Silence the violence," and chanted, "Divided we fall, united we rise!"

Slowly, neighbors came outside to see the acts of peace passing by their doors.

"It's cool," said Joanna Leon, holding her three-year-old daughter, Jocelyn. "It's a good cause. You read the newspaper and that's all you hear about — kids getting shot."

Richard Sanchez, a thirty-two-year-old electrician and former gang member, was on hand to tell young people about the consequences of fighting for a color. He spent eight years of his life "in and out" of jail. His last sentence lasted two years for shooting into a crowd of people.

When Sanchez was released, Flores — his friend from middle school — met him and offered a different path.

"When I got out of jail, all the homeboys were going in," Sanchez said. "Now, when I think back — dang, what was I thinking about then?"

One fourteen-year-old San Jose boy stands at a crossroad in his life. Though he attended Unity Day II, he admitted he's part of a gang. Still, he wore a white T-shirt, the color Flores asked everyone to wear on Saturday.

"I'm trying to change. I'm trying to get away from that," said the slender teen, who this newspaper is not identifying to protect his safety. The boy, who has a gentleness about him, said a rival gang member once pulled out a gun.

"I'm still used to the gang life. All my brothers and cousins are in it. All your enemies know. All the schools I went to know," he said. "If I see my enemies, do I let them fly or ... it's kind of hard."

The Model:

As part of my vision for The Corazón Project, I inspired the City to give gun-buy backs another chance after almost a decade of giving up on their impact. I explained that I wanted to do something different. I wanted to trade gang attire and gang paraphernalia and weapons, from pocket knives, to guns, even toy guns and violent video games, and real bullets in exchange for gift cards to various places such as: restaurants, coffee, gasoline, grocery stores, toy stores, movie tickets, etc. And to everybody's surprise it was a huge success. Over 400 gang related items (ie: bandanas, clothing) and weapons were turned in, including pocket knives and at least dozens of guns.

Along with the Unity Days, I thought the youth in my Deep Circle classes job readiness skills, assigned them community service hours teaching elementary kids how to read and they also spoke to their local middle school kids that were in after school detention about what choices they regretted during high school. My mentees also participated in community murals that contained positive messages for younger kids to chew on daily.

Corazón Project Mural

Final products of "Murals with a Message" paintings by neighborhood teens, kids, and adult volunteers as part of The Corazón Project

"Quote Motto of the Corazón Project"

136

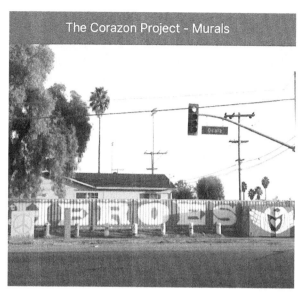

"On the left: Dave Cortese, future State Senator, Governor, President, and mentor of mine. On the right: Enrique Flores, Founder of The Corazón Project. Enrique Flores describing the progress of a mural and describing the success of each youth participant."

Writing exercise 22: What are your goals/wishes/ dreams to accomplish before the end of this year? What are your goals/wishes/dreams in the next 3 years? What are your goals/wishes/dreams in the next 5 years? How badly do you want these goals? What or who stands in your way?

MY BIRD POEM

The sun is getting ready for bed-
Time moves slow, almost stands-
Still I sit watching-
My back feels tense, my heart lone-
Some might feel afraid on the East-
Sideways I look-
Around me are the empty chairs out-
Doors open to go inside Star-
Bucks bucks paying for my
Hot chocolate tastes
Sweet on my tongue's
Tip the cup us a drink.

Then I hear it:
Chiuchi!, Chi!, Chi!, Chi!, Chiuchi!, Chi!
Birds chirping loudly!, Everybody turned around
To see what the commotion is.
I turn into a tiny black birds flying in a hurry,
Arriving to a big green tree.
The birds fly over my head, from all around,
Responding to the call!
Chiuchi!, Chi!, Chiuchi!, Chi! Chiuchi!

For five minutes now, they keep arriving, nonstop!

So, I think to myself, worried:

"Is it a fight?" - amongst birds? Are they cheering on the fight?

Chiuchi!, Chi!, Chiuchi!, Chi! Chii!

Or are they trying to stop them??

Chiuchi!, Chi!, Chi!!

"Is it an abundance of food a fellow bird found?"

"Are they all scared because an earthquake is coming? And they are terrified,

coming together to hide?"

Chiuchi!! Chi!!Chi! Chi!!

(Birds keep coming, flying to the tree, inside of the fly in, from different sky directions.)

Chiuchi!! Chi!! Chi! Chi!!- the call sounds.

More birds fly in, in a rush - top speed.

"Is it a momma-bird yelling that one of her baby-bird is not breathing?!?

Chiuchi!! Chi!!Chi! Chi!! Chiuchi!! Chi!!Chi!

But no.......

They keep chirping....

It's been 10 minutes now,

and beautiful birds keep coming, not a single moment of silence.

Chiuchi!! Chi!!Chi! Chi!! Chiuchi!! Chi!!Chi!

I first there was 50 birds in that tree easy,

then twelve more, 10 more, two more, eight more, three more, they keep flying in,

how do they all fit in there?

They must be sitting side-by-side, wing to wing, on every branch.

The chirping continues:

Chi!!Chi! Chi!! Chiuchi!! Chi!!Chi!

But they are too happy to be mourning or afraid,

then it hits me:

a nest of baby birds have hatched!! And they are all coming to celebrate and welcome them to the new world! Come in a hurry to see it!,

Excited and happy they all sound, chirping non-stop.

Chi!!Chi! Chi!! Chiuchi!! Chi!!Chi!

"But are the special babies?"

There are so many birds in the tree,

over 200 easy,

for over 20 minutes the birds fly in, none left, none came out of the tree.

"Do they do this at every birth?"

"Is it the Messiah-bird??,

The baby-God they have been waiting for?, To save them?

To bring them happiness—the leader they have hope
for, for so long, to end their suffering?
Chi!!Chi! Chi!! Chiuchi!! Chi!!Chi!
I feel excited too,
curious about the commotion.

I noticed the sun has set,
it is getting dark,
the birds keep chirping, chiuchi, chi.
but I need to study.

Writing exercise 23: Do you believe animals have souls? Do you believe souls come back over and over again until that soul reaches enlightenment? Who do you think you were in a previous life? And what type of person or animal would you like to come back in your next life?

"L WISE 1"

The following quotes have helped me to stay in the right frame of mind.

- *"The cheapest way to improve your looks is to wear a smile."* — African Proverb
- *"Más vale solo, que mal acompañado"* — Mexican Proverb
- *"Rules are for the obedience of fools and the guidance of wise men."* — Harry Day
- *"It is better to light a single candle than to curse the darkness."* — Eleanor Roosevelt
- *"Nobody is perfect. That's why pencils have erasers."* — Wolfgang Riebe
- *"My life is in the hands of any fool who makes me lose my temper."* — Joseph Hunter
- *"Procrastination is the thief of time."* — Edward Young
- *"Eagles don't take flight lessons from chickens."* — Ibhubesi the Great
- *"Problems are only opportunities with thorns on them."* — Hugh Miller
- *"When you stop chasing the wrong things, you allow the right things to catch up to you."* — Lolly Daskal

- *"The individual who says it is not possible should*

144

move out of the way of those doing it."—Tricia Cunningham

- "The only man who never makes mistakes is the man who never does anything."—Theodore Roosevelt

- "There are always two choices. Two paths to take. One is easy. And its only reward is that it's easy."—Unknown

- "The best way to destroy an enemy is to make him a friend."—Abraham Lincoln

Writing exercise 24: Choose your three favorite quotes from the previous section. Why are those your favorite? Are they speaking to you? Did those quotes pick you? Are you ready to changes, to allow yourself to be transformed into a new you?

Chapter 8

The solution begins

There was once a giant mural painting painted on the huge break wall. There were four scenes. The first section had a mighty Aztec warrior, with the shield and a large wooden stick with sharp rocks attached. The second section featured a fearless Mexican soldier, with a bullets belt across his chest holding a rifle. The third section had a pachuco with his zoot suit and a switch blade in his hand and a cane ready for combat. And lastly, there was an ordinary Chicano, down below in a cholo-squat, holding and reading a book. And the title of this painting read up above, "Weapons of War"....

In summary, this is not the conclusion of this book, but the foundation and beginning of your new life.

"Dreams don't just come true. They are built!—Enrique Flores

"We cannot think our way - into a new way of living; We need to live our way -into a new way of thinking." —Father "G-dog" Boyle, S.J.

"Once social change begins, it cannot be reversed.

You could not an uneducate a person who has learned to read,

nor humiliate the person who feels pride,

Nor oppress the people who are not afraid anymore." —Cesar Chavez

Another mentor of mine, Bob, said to me, "I want to sponsor your books. I'm going to purchase 100 copies of your memoir: *Barrio Side Hero* and I'm going to purchase 100 copies of your novel: *Kankin's Kingdom Foreseen* for every school library and every college library and every city library in the cities of San Jose and Milpitas. Bob further said, "Your first published book represents your past, what you've overcome. But the second published book, your novel, represents your future because you freed your imagination to create your future."

And I took his mentor-advice to heart, I pondered over his wise words and I decided to boldly chase my long-time unspoken dream of seeing my book made into a feature film movie. Ever since I was fifteen years old, I fell in love with movies, because going to the movie theatre saved my life. To avoid the violence in my neighborhood and in my city, especially on weekends, I would go by myself to the Capitol movie theatres or the Berryessa movie theatres at 10am when they opened and I would buy a movie ticket for a 4pm movie and I would walk in. I would go straight into the arcade and then I would sneak into other movies and watch two full movies before my purchased movie started. Before I recruited real life mentors, my mentors were all the heroes on the movie screen, Denzel Washington, Brad Pitt, Matt Damon, Mark Wahlberg, Will Smith, and others. Right now, my novel: <u>Kankin's Kingdom Foreseen</u> is being converted into a screenplay format in hopes that a Hollywood Director sees the winning horse that I see and believe, because

"Dreams don't have deadlines." —LL Cool J.

Writing exercise 25: After reading this workbook: "The Solo Cholo University"—Write anything you want about any subject. This is what is called "Free Writing". There's no right or wrong topic. Just , write whatever you want, whatever is in your head, whatever is in your heart. Don't think about it too much, just write. If you get stuck, list out what you need to STOP doing, START doing, KEEP doing, do LESS of, and do MORE of, starting today.

Made in the USA
Monee, IL
27 July 2021